Leonltale

Home Spun

Also by Leon Hale

Fiction
Bonney's Place
Addison

Non-Fiction
Turn South at the Second Bridge
A Smile From Katie Hattan
Easy Going
One Man's Christmas
Texas Chronicles

Memoir
Paper Hero

Home Spun

A Collection

LEON HALE

WINEDALE PUBLISHING
Houston

Published by
WINEDALE PUBLISHING
P.O. Box 130220   Houston, TX 77219-0220

Library of Congress Catalog Number 97-60943
ISBN 0-9657468-2-8

Book Design: Harriet Correll

Manufactured in the United States of America
First Edition

For Babette, who rescued me.

Contents

HOME SPUN

Introduction

What we have between these covers are reprints of seventy-six newspaper columns I wrote for the *Houston Chronicle* between 1989 and '96. During those seven years I did more than a thousand pieces and the seventy-six were chosen from that stack. Doing the choosing was a serious chore.

Three previous collections of the column have been published. A book reviewer commented on one of those as being a "distillation" of my work. When we were struggling through the selection process for this volume, I thought wistfully about the fantasy the reviewer's comment produced in my head—that we might dump the thousand-plus clippings into some kind of hopper and light a fire under the boiler and presently seven years of work would be distilled to a few pieces suitable for preservation in a book. The remainder would be mulch we could scatter over the flower beds.

A wonderful notion. But the reality is that a team of readers, ranging in age from the mid-twenties to mid-seventies, spent weeks separating from the stack the pieces they thought were strong enough for the collection. Then re-reading, changing their minds, throwing back what they'd chosen. Then re-reading again, and maybe retrieving what they'd discarded, and getting together, finally, to debate their selections. The throwing out and the taking back were going on right up to the final day, when the deadline made us stop.

You may notice that we haven't organized the book into categories, the way previous collections of mine have been. The reason for this is that we wanted to give new readers a sense of what it's like to read the column regularly, with a different category of subject matter each day. For others, however, we've included in the back a list of stories, by subject. If long-time customers want to see if one of their favorite columns is included, that list should be helpful.

The pieces in this collection appear as they ran in the paper, except for minor editing to make them fit more smoothly into a book format. In two cases we combined a number of columns that ran originally as series—"Normandy" beginning on page 163, and the story of "Primavera" on page 89.

Regular readers of the column will be familiar with the names and places that keep popping up in this book, but new customers might need some background. So let's have quick introductions to the fortune teller—Madame Z—and to My Friend Mel, Old Friend Morgan, the country house in Washington County, and the neighborhood ice house. Also to the person frequently referred to as my partner.

My partner is a woman, and my bride. We were associated in a modest business partnership several years before we married, so my calling her partner was comfortable for us both then and still is. For a reason I can't quite explain, it's traditional for newspaper columnists to refer in print to spouses as something other than wife or husband.

My partner and I bought the country house in Washington County as an investment before we got married and use it now as a quiet place to run to when the walls of the city begin moving in, pressing us. The house lies about ninety miles northwest of Houston. It's not a farm, and certainly not a ranch. It covers 10.7 acres of oak, cedar, trashy brush and native grass. Sometimes we're asked what we raise on this vast acreage. The answer is, fire ants, grasshoppers, armadillos, poison ivy, and a few antique roses. We could manage that on a lot fewer than 10.7 acres but we have these two Labrador dogs that need room to range, and find smelly things to roll in.

I do an occasional day's work at the old place and the customers sometimes think we live there. No. Parts of that four-room frame house were nailed together almost one hundred and fifty years ago and it leaks on rainy days and grunts and moans on windy nights and that's fine now and then on weekends when we're feeling adventurous. But not as a steady diet. The place has two saving graces, though. One is the fifty-five-foot front porch, which on mild days is a great spot to work, or to watch the sun go down and wait for the coyotes to sing. The other is a stand of splendid live oaks, middle-aged and healthy. They surround the house, almost as if they're holding it up, and these trees make the place special for us.

One of the guests we've had there is My Friend Mel (see "City Boy", page 146), who didn't like it and left early. He is just what I call him, a friend named Mel, a fellow who comes around now and then to visit and drink coffee and give advice and criticism that I don't want or need. I retaliate by taking to him, to be repaired, anything mechanical of mine that goes on the blink. Mel has a shopful of tools and can fix things, which I cannot. We have been friends for thirty years and though we seldom agree on any question, if I ended up in jail in the middle of the night, Mel is one of the guys I would call, and he would come get me out.

So would Old Friend Morgan, my *compadre* in the *Primavera* adventure. On page 185 he tells the "Pretty Horse" story, which may be my favorite piece in this collection. O.F.

and I are friends due to an accidental meeting of the least likely sort. In the early fifties I was introduced to Morgan when he was living on the Texas coast at Freeport. It was one of those shake-and-glad-to-meet-you introductions, after which you turn away and expect never to see one another again.

About five years later I was walking unsteadily along *Paseo de la Reforma* in Mexico City, dizzy from the altitude sickness that often affects flatland visitors there. I was in Mexico on assignment and I was not only sick but a week late in my work because I was frustrated in my attempt to contact the sources I needed. I was waiting on a traffic light, holding onto a pole like a drunk, and I heard somebody call my name.

It was O.F. All those millions of people milling in the streets of Mexico's capital, and Morgan happened to walk across *Reforma* at that moment to see me hanging onto a pole. He was living down there. His fluent Spanish had gotten him a position procuring materials for a mining operation his company was planning in Coahuila, and which he would later manage. In Mexico that day he separated me from that pole. Got me doctored. Set up my appointments. Interpreted my interviews. Saved my bacon.

That was the first of many stories we have since worked on together, most of them with a Mexican flavor and a need for Morgan's Spanish. I do this sort of thing for a living. O.F. has done it for fun, not only in Mexico but back home, too, after his retirement. And not just for me but for other scribes who wander into his territory, needing help. He lives now in the little Texas coastal town of Sweeny.

My fortune teller friend, Madame Z, lives on the west bank of the Brazos River within a few hours drive of Houston, but I mustn't be more specific than that. Madame is a recluse and does not welcome visitors, not even those willing to pay her to tell their fortunes. She long ago retired from the fortune-telling game, and lives alone with her chickens and hanging baskets.

I met Madame about the same time I had that first handshake with Old Friend Morgan. Even then she called herself retired and that was forty years ago. At that time I was dedicated to seeking out the most outrageous characters hiding in remote places in Texas, and I don't mind saying I did make a noticeable dent in the total. Madame was my favorite of the bunch, and I have gone back to see her several times a year since our beginning, and written a report on what she says or does.

Two of the more frequent questions I hear about Madame have to do with her race and her age. I would say her race is mixed, and she once told me she doesn't know how old she is. "I don't remember being born," as she says. Her early time was spent in the Brazos Bottom, being passed from family to family to work on the great farms common along the river.

The fact is that Madame is not much of a fortune teller. She did travel several years with a small carnival and took the name Madame Z and sat in a tent and dealt cards and posed, at least, as a teller of fortunes. There have been vague references to some time she spent on the West Coast, dealing stud poker and other parlor games. She handles a deck of playing cards like a Las Vegas magician. Often entertains herself by playing a game of solitaire with two full decks. And she always wins.

I now see Madame five to six times a year. She seems all right. She suffers from rheumatism and life, as she puts it. She also suffers from excessively hot weather and when the day's high in the river bottom reaches ninety in the spring, she migrates to higher elevations and lower temperatures, usually somewhere in Colorado. And returns to Texas on the leading edge of the first decent cool front in October. She still cooks on a wood stove. Her favorite drink is strawberry

Kool-Aid. Her favorite food is fruitcake. Why she took the name Madame Z I don't know. Eight out of ten people who mention her to me call her Madame X. She hates being called Madame X.

Sometimes the customers wonder if Madame goes with me to the neighborhood ice house where I sometimes hang out, and try to call it work. No way. Madame wouldn't go near such a place, where all those people are. The ice house I frequent and mention in the column sometimes is a beer joint, as I suppose most people understand. I go there not so much for the beer as for the conversation from the mixture of citizens drawn into such places. Doctors, bums, judges, teachers, secretaries, cops, robbers, sometimes even socialites.

I confess my neighborhood ice house is not always the same ice house. I've never been comfortable having a public place as an office, as some columnists use a fancy restaurant or night club where the patrons parade by to get their names in print. I hear and see more of what I want to hear and see in places where people don't know what I do. And I figure that's fair enough, as long as I don't use what I learn to do anybody damage.

Maybe this is a good place to answer a couple of other questions I often hear. One is, "Do you enjoy doing the column? Is it fun?"

I love my job and have never wanted another. However, I can't say I have fun while grinding out the column because the actual writing is pretty tedious work. But when I've finished and I've produced something I like and which the customers say they enjoy reading, that's when the fun comes. Or the grief, in case I write something that's punk and which nobody likes.

The principle reward of doing a long-established column in a major publication is that so many people become interested in your work. Not so much in the columnist, but in what the columnist does. I believe the main reason for this is, readers feel they could do such a column themselves. And maybe they could. The qualifications are not very exclusive. Any literate person can turn out eight hundred words on a subject in which he or she has a passionate interest.

Whether such a person could sustain the passion, and turn out the words week after week, year after year, is another matter but many believe they could even before they've tried, and they might be right. Every year at my vacation time I get offers from readers who volunteer to fill my space, at no charge, while I'm gone. I've always said no. I'm afraid of guest columnists who want to work for nothing. They might be too good, and cause my editors to start rubbing their chins and thinking dark thoughts.

Another common query I get is, "Are you planning to retire soon?" A fair question, since I've been doing the column for close to forty-five years. The answer is no. I intend to keep on keeping on until the paper invites me to take a hike, or until I'm unable to do a day's work for whatever reason. It's mighty hard to get an old newspaper columnist to quit.

My thanks now to the *Houston Chronicle* for permission to reprint these columns. Several people were central players in the production of this book, and I am grateful for their labors. Special among them are the *Chronicle's* librarian Sherry Adams, Harriet Correll, Lori Patel, and my partner, who did most of the hard part, by far. See you on down the road.

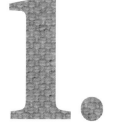

Hobby Surfing

One afternoon about forty years ago a doctor out on South Main took the blood pressure cuff off my arm and squinted at me and frowned and asked, "Do you have a hobby?"

I had to think a few seconds before I realized that sure enough I didn't. This had never occurred to me.

He said, "Is there anything you'd like to do, something you'd enjoy that might make you relax?"

I told him yes, there were dozens of things like that I wanted to do.

"Name one," he said.

The piano. I always wanted to learn to play the piano.

"Wonderful," the doctor said. "Do it. That's my advice."

Do you suppose I went forth then and took lessons and bought a piano? No, but I bought a book about learning the piano, and got the names of several piano teachers, and a time or two I even shopped around for a secondhand upright that would fit into my space.

That's as near as I've come to learning the piano.

Never mind, I switched to golf. I had a multitude of friends who loved golf. So I decided to take up the game. This was in 1960, somewhere around there.

Since then I've owned two sets of clubs and three books

about golf and I've taken a few lessons. But I've never actually gone out and played, the way normal people do. I've rehearsed some, which didn't encourage me. Friends say, "Come on and play. It doesn't matter if your game is bad."

Yes it does.

The trouble with golf is that people *look* at you when you swing. They ought to have the decency to avert their eyes. But instead they watch, and when you top the ball and it bounces out yonder thirty feet from the tee, they tell you not to worry about it.

When what they are saying to themselves is, "Oh boy, it's gonna be a long morning."

They'll tell you the same thing about bridge. I tried bridge. It's a fine game. I've got two books on bridge. Friends who love you will invite you to play and when you say you're not very good at the game they'll say, "Don't worry about that. We play for fun."

Fun, eh? Make that blood.

At one a.m. preparing to retire, the very person who invited you is muttering to her husband, "You'd think any half-wit would know that a bid of four no-trump is asking for aces."

Then I took up drawing.

I've always wanted to draw, to experience the elation that artists must feel when they make a mark with a pencil, and it comes alive. I bought a book, *Drawing on the Right Side of the Brain*, by Betty Edwards. A fine book. I recommend it. For me it didn't work but for you it might.

Next was cooking.

I loved cooking. I was about ready to give up the newspaper business and hire out to a good restaurant. Then some busybody invented cholesterol and I couldn't eat anything I cooked.

Birds were next.

Hobby Surfing

A rewarding hobby, watching birds. I bought four books on birds. I like birds. But the bird people took me out and made me squat in weeds and grass with a pair of binoculars. I was supposed to identify a singled-wattled droop-beaked rufous-winged bang-tailed chickaboo. I couldn't handle it. Not with fire ants crawling up my britches.

After birds was foreign language.

Spanish. French. German. I've got the books to prove I intended to learn how to speak them all. Did I do it? Don't ask.

Beekeeping came along in there. So did ham radio. Guitar. Drums. (I've still got sticks, and books about Gene Krupa and Buddy Rich, but I never got a drum to beat). Winemaking. Vegetable gardening.

I stayed with vegetables two years, a record for me, and I acquired half a shelf of books on gardening. I raised a crop or two of runty tomatoes up there at the old house in Washington County. Then the cottontail rabbits and the bugs and the deer put me out of business.

So I looked around to see what I had left, and it was books. I said, Hey, maybe I ought to collect books for a hobby. I called in a friend who knows about book collecting and he said, "You've got books, but you don't have any direction. You need a direction."

I've still got the books but I haven't figured out what direction I want to go as a book collector.

Meanwhile, after forty years, my blood pressure remains high. But I'm studying how to get it down. And I've got a book about it.   ∾

Homer, Come Back

*T*his story starts out entirely truthful and goes along that way for quite a few paragraphs. It's about an extraordinary rat.

Every now and then, in the house where we live, a rat gets in the attic. It chews on things and wakes us up in the middle of the night. We have spent a good deal of money sealing places we think might admit rats. Still they get in.

I bought rat traps. Industrial strength traps, the old-fashioned kind that go WHAP and a metal bar comes down and kills the rat. Except sometimes it doesn't kill the rat but only traps it and this is really not pleasant. I don't enjoy seeing rats suffer.

Also I've never been comfortable setting a trap of that sort. I'm always afraid it'll go off while I'm handling it and break a finger for me. In this business, where you work on a keyboard all the time, a broken finger is an injury of consequence. Almost be better to break a leg.

So I went to the hardware store and bought a trap that doesn't kill anything. It's a wire cage sixteen inches long and about six inches wide and six inches tall.

The literature said bait it with peanuts. You put the peanuts on a trigger pan, and set a trap door in one end of the cage.

Rat goes in, touches a peanut, and CLACK, door falls and traps that rodent.

The second night, I caught one. And I mean this was a serious rat. You could put a fuzzy tail on that thing and pass him off as a squirrel.

All right, I had a rat in my cage. I hadn't thought of what I'd do when I caught one.

Kill him? But how? Feed him poison and watch him die? Open the door and try to whack him with a stick when he runs out? Shoot him? Here in town?

"Why don't you take him somewhere and set him free?" my partner said.

I had mixed feelings about that, but I drove to Memorial Park and carried the cage back in the woods and let the rat out. He went loping into the timber toward Buffalo Bayou. Seemed to me he loped funny. One of his hind legs looked splayed, as if it might have been injured and healed.

Two days passed.

Then we heard rat-chewing noises in the attic again. I got the peanuts out of the refrigerator and set the trap. That night, CLACK, got another rat.

I noticed this second one had the same kind of splayed hind foot the first one had. Made me laugh at myself, for even thinking it might be the same rat.

But, just for fun, I opened a can of white enamel out of the storage closet and found a small brush and I dabbed that rat's tail before I took him away. With about an inch of his tail showing bright white.

This time I drove way outside the Loop on San Felipe and turned the rat loose under the Buffalo Bayou bridge a little way west of Voss. And measured the distance back home—5.1 miles.

I kept the trap baited in the attic. Nothing happened for five days. Then about four o'clock one morning, CLACK.

Climbed up to check, and there he was, looking scruffy and tired, chomping on his peanuts. The paint on his tail identified him well enough, though it was flaked and dim.

I kept him around for a couple of days and let him rest and fatten up some. Then I freshened his tail paint and named him Homer and drove him out the Katy Freeway to Texas 6 and let him loose in the parking lot of a hotel.

He got out and sniffed and looked at the sun and loped back east and was home again in eleven days.

Well, you can see why I got pretty excited about this discovery—a homing rat. Figured I might make money off him some way.

But now I've fouled up.

For the final test I carried that rat thirty miles from the house and set him down along FM 1463 south of Katy. That was three weeks ago, and I haven't heard a squeak out of him and I'm worried.

He might have got run over by a pickup, or caught by a hawk or a coyote out on that prairie. I'm asking folks west of town to watch out for my rat. He's got a splayed right hind foot and a white tail and answers to the name Homer. Give him a handful of peanuts and point him east. ∾

Inherited Mobility

My son, the happy nomad, phoned from the city of Wichita, Kansas. He wanted to know what the weather was doing here.

There is no telling why he is in Kansas but I will give you better than even money he won't be there long, because of this early winter we're getting. He is opposed to winter, and runs from cold fronts as if they might carry poisonous fumes. He once moved from Mobile down to St. Petersburg because he couldn't stand the bitter winters of Alabama. So I expect in the next couple of weeks he will pass through Houston, going south. Dragging his house behind him.

He mentioned Brownsville as a possible destination. What he wants is a place where he can play golf without a shirt on New Year's Day.

The last time he passed this way he was driving a three-quarter ton truck, a handsome and sturdy machine, but I did wonder why a guy who keeps on the move wouldn't want a softer-riding vehicle. He said the house trailer is thirty feet long so he needs power to pull it. That's how I learned about the trailer.

I've not seen it yet but I know what it looks like and I can visualize its interior, decorated with his organized clutter. I knew, from the time he was about twenty-five, that he'd end up with a house on wheels, and that he'd be a wanderer.

He inherited the tendency, the same as he got blue eyes, big feet, and a lust for Tex-Mex enchiladas. If you are a parent who has produced one or more of these nomads, you might as well lean back and relax. Because you're not going to change them.

This guy's grandfather, my father, had a chronic case of the itching foot. He scratched that itch all the way to the end. He never bought a house. That was too much like staying forever put. He preferred renting. Renting meant that on the first of the month he could tell the landlord he was leaving, and go somewhere else. I think what he liked even better was a hotel, where he could check out and leave at any time.

Every year I see my son growing more and more like his grandfather. I have learned to be pleased by this. If my father knew this was happening, he would enter into a state of exaltation. It's like his life, the way he dreamed it could be, is being lived by his grandson.

It warms my insides to imagine these two together, going down the road in that truck with their house trailing behind them. Not knowing where they're headed and not much caring, but eager to see what lies beyond the next hill.

They would get along first rate. The grandfather would not find anything strange about the habits of his grandson.

When he stops to see me now, he arrives about the time I'm eating breakfast. That means he has traveled all night. Unless he's driving through new country where he needs to see the land, he'll get on the road about ten p.m. and keep going until sunrise. His grandfather would have no problem with that. No words had greater appeal to my father than these: "Hey, let's go, right now."

My father would love that house trailer. Bedrooms. Bathroom. Kitchen. Heat and air conditioning. And all those beautiful wheels underneath. Plus a TV set in the living room, with a remote channel changer. A zapper, I call it.

I can't watch TV with my son if he is in control of the zapper. Because he watches four or five channels at once, and zaps constantly from one to the other, and it makes me batty.

We'll be watching the Oilers, say, and they've got third and seven inside Pittsburgh's twenty and Moon pedals back in the shotgun and throws and some guy from the New York Jets intercepts.

Which can't be, because we're playing Pittsburgh, and I need a minute to see that we've changed channels and we're watching the Jets vs. Miami. So I adjust to this new game, and the Jets run two plays and suddenly we're watching a stock car race in Florida or somewhere, and I surrender and go back to the office and read.

But my father? He would dearly love that channel switching. He used to do it on the radio. He listened to the radio with one hand on the tuning dial, and wandered from station to station, and I think that for him it was a way of traveling, being forever on the move from one place to another.

(Author's note: I wrote this piece before I learned why my son was in Kansas. Her name is Victoria and she has since become the mother of two of my grandchildren.)   ∽

Blame the Fruitcake

*W*hat did it was the fruitcake. Up until then, I was doing all right. But that one bite of cake began a chain reaction, and the damage has been extensive.

I shouldn't have brought any kind of cake in the house, but I did, about the middle of December. Ten small fruitcakes, sized for individuals. A cake that fits in the palm of the hand. I bought them to give away. They make nice little Christmas presents and don't cost much.

Those cakes were around the house for a week, out of sight in their neat packaging, and they didn't bother me until I got ready to give them away. That was the day I said to Myself, "You at least ought to taste one. How else will you know whether they're any good?"

Myself replied, "Don't do it. Remember your pledge. This is going to be the holiday season when you don't eat any sweet, rich, party food. You can do it if you just won't start."

"Come on," I argued with Myself. "One little piece of cake won't hurt anything."

Myself said, "Yes, it will, too. You won't be able to stop, and before you're through you'll eat everything that's bad for you and by New Year's Day your cholesterol count will look like the U.S. trade deficit."

"Don't be such an old grinch," I told Myself, and un-wrapped the little cake and ate every crumb of it.

That afternoon a friend sent us a package of beautiful shelled pecans. I'm not sure, but I think I ate them all. They're gone, anyway.

And that night, before I went to bed, I fixed a large mug of vanilla ice cream with coffee liqueur poured over it. I haven't done such a thing in two years. I used to do it every night, long ago, before the medical profession got meddlesome about what we eat.

Anyhow, that was the first day and now I am out of control.

All those calories may have me hallucinating. We went to this party and I wandered in where they had all the food laid out and I saw a great round platter covered with carrot sticks, arranged in a splendid geometric pattern. I ate three or four, after dipping them in a bowl of non-fat yogurt. I told Myself, "I have never tasted carrot sticks as good as these, especially when dipped in this non-fat yogurt."

Myself replied, "Those are not carrot sticks. They're ched-dar cheese, which has a fat content exceeded only by that quote unquote non-fat yogurt, which is not yogurt at all but creamy onion dip."

But by then I had stopped listening to Myself, and in an-other day or two he quit talking altogether. I was thankful he shut up, or went away, or whatever happened to him, because I would hate to hear what he'd say about the eggnog.

Yes, I did it. I have sunk that low into a caloric, fat-laden, salt-shaken Christmas. I went out and bought two quarts of supermarket eggnog mix and brought it home and drank cup after cup of it with bourbon whiskey stirred in.

Then finally I quit putting in the whiskey because it tends to hide the flavor of the eggnog.

I confess I had forgotten how good all this sinful holiday

food tastes. I used to wonder why we eat so much party junk, but that was before I got separated from it. I see now why we do it. It tastes so fine, that's why.

Listen to this—fried mozzarella cheese fingers. There's one I'd never met before. I ate at least two hands of those things—ten fingers. Then I was introduced to quiche tarts. They're made of eggs and bacon and cheese and the Devil Himself knows what else. I kept at these tarts until I felt a gentle but firm hand at my elbow, telling me to move along, move along, go to the celery sticks.

But I don't want celery sticks, not this week. Now that I'm settled in on this bender, I avoid healthful food. Because I know that after New Year's Day I'll be back on green salads and grilled fish until my numbers at the clinic come back down out of the red paint. May take until next Thanksgiving. You pay a price for binges like this.

But today, go ahead, pile it on: Give me giblet gravy on my cornbread dressing. Give me butter on my rolls. Give me rum cake with ice cream on the side. Give me fudge. Chocolate cookies. Creamy dips. Salty chips.

Fruitcake? You think I'd want more of what set me off on this food bender? I would. But now I want a generous slop of whipped cream on top.

I'll pay the price next year, but right now I don't want anything to eat unless it's bad for me. ❧

He's Pro-Coyote

*I*t's five-thirty p.m. on the front porch of the old country house in Washington County. I'm sitting here celebrating the close of a splendid day, and waiting for the coyotes to sing.

Judging from the serenades we've heard on recent evenings, the coyotes have passed a favorable summer, and raised lots and lots of new voices. Because we have detected renewed vigor in the choir.

Here on this small reservation we happen to be pro-coyote, which is probably a minority position, and so we are careful what we say about those wily canines. When we visit neighbors, I mean, in local taverns, and country stores, and other places where the subject of coyotes is apt to come up.

I don't think anybody has ever bothered to do it, but the population hereabouts could be divided into two broad groups—pro-coyote, and anti-coyote.

The anti-coyoters are likely to be the longtime rural people who have worked their land for generations and are still raising things that coyotes like to kill and eat, such as domestic free-ranging poultry. To these people, the coyote is the enemy, the same as hawks, and snakes, and bad weather, and trespassers who leave gates open.

The pro-coyoters are apt to be weekenders, people like us

who live and work in the city and keep a modest amount of rural real estate, not to raise domestic poultry or anything else, but mainly as places to escape the congestion of cities.

We like to feel we are in the wilderness, far from freeways and office hours, and the coyote helps us achieve that notion. Its song is the wildest sound we hear, and we love it. We want coyotes closer than they come. We'd prefer them to trot through the front gate and point their muzzles at the moon and render a chorus or two right here inside the yard fence.

We have city friends who don't believe us when we talk about sitting on the porch and hearing the coyotes howl. They suppose coyotes are all gone from Texas, along with dinosaurs and timber wolves and buffalo and ivory billed woodpeckers.

We have made the mistake of inviting people to come spend a night with us, so they can hear coyotes howl for the first time. But coyotes are contrary animals and will, almost without fail, refuse to open their mouths when company is here and waiting for a performance.

I have known landowners in these parts to cross over, and change their position relative to coyotes. The change is always from pro to anti. This happens when one of these weekend station wagon farmers decides to try raising a few pullets. He wants the experience of going out to the chicken house before breakfast and gathering fresh-laid eggs from the nest.

Then one morning he goes forth and discovers all he's got left of his pullets is enough feathers to stuff a sofa, plus a ton of coyote tracks. Immediately the guy becomes an anti-coyoter, and remains one forever.

These converts are fierce and dedicated and often go around proselytizing among the pros, bringing us stories of the latest coyote felonies. They tell me, for example, the reason there's not a covey of quail on this place is that ground-nesting birds don't survive the night raids of coyotes.

Then the most recent and disturbing report has coyotes spreading rabies in South Texas and threatening the health of unvaccinated pets, and therefore the safety of humans as well.

A bad business indeed, if true, and when the coyotes in these woods around here begin attacking yard dogs, maybe I'll cross over too, and become an anti.

So coyotes have become a sort of social problem, and a delicate subject like politics or religion or abortion. Right now I remain pro-coyote, but I'm pro-choice in social situations. What I mean, I'm not mad at anybody who's against coyotes. Some of my best friends are anti-coyoters, and in fact my sister married one.

Almost four hours have passed since I sat down here to wait and listen. It's a perfect night, star-lit and calm, and I know the coyotes are out there because when they're near the dogs are quiet and stay up on the porch. No serenade, though. Not a note. Being a friend to coyotes is not getting any easier. ❧

They Might Not Look Mean

At our neighborhood ice house the television set above the bar finally stopped rolling and went dark and silent. As sometimes happens in this situation, one of the regulars opened the newspaper and started reading a story aloud, like a TV announcer.

The reader was a young woman known as Dakota, because she comes from way up around Bismarck, and it was a story about child abuse. When she finished the story she said, "I wonder what kind of people would do that to a little kid. I don't believe I've ever seen anybody who looked evil enough to do such things."

Silence for a moment, and then the one they call T-Shirt made a rumble in his throat and said: "Well, they might not look mean. They might look okay, and still be mean as snakes."

Dakota asked him, "You sound like you had experience with people like that."

T-Shirt produced a sort of snort and said, "How about I was raised by one. Leastways partly, until I got sense enough to run away from him."

"Your daddy?" somebody asked.

"Naw. Wasn't no kin of mine. He was my stepmama's boyfriend."

T-Shirt got that nickname because of his style of dress. He always comes to the ice house wearing khaki pants, black belt, white crew neck T-shirt, black shoes, white socks. In cold weather he'll put on a light jacket.

He has a round German-looking face, short graying hair, heavy shoulders, stocky body. He looks so clean. Khakis pressed. Shoes gleaming. Face red from a fresh shave. T-Shirt must be pushing sixty. He talks sometimes about being in Korea before he was twenty.

"Your stepmother's boyfriend," Dakota said to him. "What happened to your mother?"

"Died," T-Shirt said, "when I was a baby. I don't hardly remember her, except she had long black hair. My daddy married again pretty soon after. Edna, my stepmama."

"And she was mean?" somebody asked.

"Edna? Naw. She was a pussycat. When I was about eight, my daddy showed up missin'. Went off one night and didn't come home. Never did. Right now I don't know what happened to him. Like as not he's dead by this time. Next year or two me and Edna did all right. She got her a job slingin' hash, and kept me in school, and then she come home with that Gilbert. He spent the night and never did leave."

A shadowy figure appeared and set a fresh longneck in front of T-Shirt, and withdrew. This happens at the ice house when somebody is telling a personal story. The beer is a token of assurance. It says, "Thanks for sharing this experience, and please go on." Nobody would ever speak those words, but they are understood.

"At first," T-Shirt said, "I liked him all right, you know? I mean I was missin' my daddy and Gilbert would get out and knock me flies, and we went fishin' some. But he didn't do right. Supposed to be a carpenter but he wouldn't ever work.

"The rough stuff started one night, I guess he was drinkin'. We were at the supper table and I asked for the syrup and he drew back his arm and caught me a lick across the mouth and his ring cut me, I still got this scar, eight stitches.

"After that it seemed like he got his kicks out of hurtin' me. Used to come in my room and beat on me with a board, and Edna standin' there beggin' him to stop. He'd lock me out of the house sometimes on cold nights.

"He bought one of these electric cattle prods, like they use to haze cows through pens and chutes? He'd catch me in the bathtub and jab me with that thing, and it hurt bad. He was good at punchin' me on my back and belly where it wouldn't show when I had my clothes on. I still got scars here, on the inside of my legs, where he held me down one time and branded me with a hot poker out of the fireplace. And there was other stuff I couldn't tell you about, because I don't like to say it.

"One day, I was almost fifteen, I got Edna off and I told her I was cuttin' out, and she ought to go with me, or else call the law on Gilbert. And you know what? She wouldn't go. She wouldn't call the law, either.

"I picked my night and walked away from there, and made it on my own until I signed up in the Army, and I still wonder why Edna stayed with that guy. He was a good-looking fellow, but he was sure mean.

"You can't ever tell anything," T-Shirt said, "by the way they look." ∾

Rescuing Christina's Cat

*M*onday morning my friend Mel called me from Pueblo, Colo. and said he needed some help in rescuing a cat.

"Christina and I are up here on a trip," he said, "and last night Christina's cat got out and climbed a tree and won't come down. It looks like rain, so I need your help."

Wait a second now. Did he want me to go all the way to Pueblo to help him get a cat out of a tree?

"No, no," he said. "The cat's not here, it's there, at our house, in the top of the mulberry tree in the front yard."

I wondered how he knew, if he was in Colorado, that the cat is up a tree in Houston. And how he knew it looked like rain here, which Monday morning it did.

"Mrs. Withers," Mel said. "She's our neighbor across the street and one door to the right. She's feeding the cat while we're gone, and last night it got out and she called us, and she called back this morning, twice, and she's pretty frantic."

So why doesn't Mrs. Withers get the cat out of the tree?

"Because she can't climb," Mel said. "She's got rheumatism or something, and she might fall."

I told him all the cats I ever knew were able to climb down anything they climbed up.

"You don't know this cat, though," Mel said. "It's been up there before, and it won't come down without getting rescued. Christina's afraid it'll get struck by lightning if a storm comes."

Struck by lightning? No cat on Earth has ever been struck by lightning.

"This one would do it, though," Mel said, "out of spite, just to give me grief. Listen, there's something you have to know. Before you bring the cat down, you've got to catch the dog."

The dog? What dog?

"Belongs to the Baileys, next door to Mrs. Withers. Runs around the neighborhood all the time. I don't know what kind. Black and white and shaggy. He chased the cat up the mulberry tree when Mrs. Withers let it get loose. No way that cat'll come down while the dog's still in the yard."

Why don't the Baileys come out to catch their own dog?

"Because they're not home. They're down on Padre Island somewhere. Practically everybody on the block's gone, except Mrs. Withers. That's why I called you. Wait a minute. Christina's trying to tell me something . . . oh. She says the dog's name is Beetle."

Beetle Bailey. That's real cute. What am I supposed to do with Beetle Bailey if I catch him?

"Tie him up, I guess. Put him in your car until you get the cat down. But listen, try not to touch him."

Catch him but don't touch him. That'll be a trick. Why not?

"Because if you touch him, his scent will be on your hands and the cat won't let you get anywhere close. You'll need a ladder, too, and you'll have to get my ladder out of Milton Fuller's garage because he borrowed it and hasn't brought it back."

And where might Milton Fuller live? In Sioux City?

"No, two doors down from Mrs. Withers, toward the school. She can let you in the Fullers' garage because she has a key so she can feed their parakeets while they're gone to a wedding in Shreveport."

All right, what else?

"Well, Christina says remember this cat's not used to anybody but her. She says after you catch the dog, go in our back bathroom and wash your hands with her soap, which is the pink bar, and that way you'll smell a little like *her*, and maybe the cat will be easier to catch. She says hold your hand out to it and let it sniff. But the main thing is, you've got to keep calling its name."

So what's its name?

"You won't like it," Mel said.

Told him I didn't expect to like it.

"Sweet Stuff," he said.

Heaven send us mercy.

When he hung up, I sat a while and wondered: Was I really about to drive halfway across town and lasso a strange dog named Beetle Bailey and fetch a ladder out of a house I'd never seen and wash my hands in perfumed soap and climb up a tree calling, "Here, Sweet Stuff . . . here, Sweet Stuff . . . ?" Shouldn't there be limits on what you make yourself do in public, even for friends?

Before I got out of my chair, Mel called again, sounding bright. "Guess what, pal, you're off the hook. Mrs. Withers just called back. There was a big clap of thunder, and Sweet Stuff came out of the tree like a flying squirrel and hit the ground about twice and shot in the house and under the sofa, so he's home safe."

I have been sitting here trying to decide whether this event had a beneficiary, and I believe now it did—the telephone company. Six long distance calls between Texas and Colorado, generated by a cat in the top of a mulberry tree. Only in America.   ❧

Monkeyshines

$\mathcal{H}$ere is a letter from my Cousin C.T., who asks if I remember the time I got in trouble by hitting Uncle Burl Moody on the head with a ripe cantaloupe.

Maybe the regular customers will remember Cousin C.T., who gets a mention here now and then. In my barefoot years I spent several summers on the farm where C.T. and his family lived, and where I learned many lessons in how to waste time.

C.T. was my teacher. He was a little older than I was, and therefore I was obliged to listen to his opinions and respect his judgments, for in those days the world operated on seniority.

He did know things of value that I needed to learn. Most of them could be filed under the heading of monkey business, but monkey business was important then to people of our age and our standing.

Reason for the importance was C.T.'s father, a strict master who wanted everybody working, all the time.

Boys at play were an abomination in that man's sight. It is my honest belief that he got physical pain from seeing boys running foot races for fun, or wrestling in the dust, or chunking rocks at lizards. I believe a voice said to him, about the sight of children at play, "What a waste of energy. They could be chopping cotton, or slopping the hogs."

So, if you wanted any fun on that farm, you had to have it out of C.T.'s father's sight. And that's how we did it.

If he told us, "Now I want you boys to go over yonder in the back pasture and find that old bald-face cow with the crooked horn. She hasn't come up in three days. I want to know if she's got a calf yet."

Which was a good assignment because it didn't have a time limit. Finding that old cow might take hours, and we could roam for miles and call it hunting for the cow.

We could go to the creek and swim, and chunk water moccasins, and smoke a little grapevine, and C.T. would give lessons in monkey business. How to catch a locust and put it in your shirt pocket and tap it and make it buzz on command. How to walk through brush and catch hold of a limb and bend it and let it go so it would give a slap in the stomach to a person following close behind. How to skeet a flat rock across a stock tank. Things like that. Valuable stuff.

Concerning the matter of hitting Uncle Burl Moody with the cantaloupe, that came about due to C.T.'s idea to bomb the chickens from the hay loft.

In late summer the watermelons and the cantaloupes left in the field would get close to worthless—all sun scalded or overripe and shriveled. C.T.'s father would send us to the field with wheelbarrows to pick those bad melons and cantaloupes and bring 'em in and feed 'em to the hogs.

Not a lot of fun, so C.T. devised this game. We chose a supply of nice soft cantaloupes, close to the edge of rotten, and took them up in the hay loft for ammunition.

Then we got an ear of corn out of the crib and scattered kernels on the ground just below the hay loft door, to draw the hens. These were big old Rhode Island Reds that lay those brown eggs you pay extra for now.

Idea was to drop cantaloupes out of the loft and see who

could hit a hen on the ground. This was the sort of monkey business that appealed to most male youths of that time, and you see the same appeal living today in their grandchildren—kids zapping targets in computer games.

You needn't worry that we hurt the chickens. I don't recall any direct hits, but we enjoyed some near misses that caused explosions of flapping and squawking, and that was the idea, anyhow, to cause a satisfactory racket.

What we didn't know was that Uncle Burl Moody was in the barn fixing harness and walked out front to see what the hens were squawking about, and that's when I was making a drop and my cantaloupe got him.

But not on the head, as C.T. said in his letter. It hit him a glancing shot on the shoulder. It was a soft cantaloupe that couldn't have hurt much, but it did draw out of him some extraordinary language I'd never heard him use before.

To answer the question in the letter, yes, I remember the event well, since Uncle Burl didn't have any more patience with monkey business than C.T.'s father. And maybe less. ∾

He Needs a Tractor

So here we are again at the old country house in Washington County where I have been busy for two days, trying to keep from buying a tractor.

Two problems are involved in this matter. One is that I want a tractor pretty bad. I want one worse than I wanted the old pickup before I got that.

The other problem is that my partner is not as enthusiastic about tractors as I am. If I get one, it will be half hers according to the rules of the partnership, as well as the community property laws of this state. So she has been asking delicate tractor questions.

Such as, "Why do we need one?"

Well, if she would pay attention she would see that all our neighbors around here have a tractor, and some have two. Does she want us to be the only tractorless people in South Washington County?

"But what would we do with a tractor?" she asked. "You're not going to plow, are you?"

No, but I could shred.

Shred. What a magnificent word. Shredding, as some of the city customers may not know, is kin to mowing but it's not in the same league. Mowing is to shredding what water is to whiskey.

What you do is hook up a shredder to the power takeoff of a tractor and you attack tall stands of weeds and you make mulch out of those babies. The knife-sharp rotary blades revolve at a tremendous speed and the destruction they cause is frightening and wonderful.

You turn around in your tractor seat and look back where you've shredded and those weeds are *slain*, man, and you can smell the sap.

"But how many times a year," she asked, "would you need to shred? Maybe twice? And you're going to buy an expensive tractor and use it only twice a year?"

I said I hoped she'd credit me with more sense than that. Of course I wouldn't buy a tractor and use it only twice a year. A tractor has many uses on a place like this.

"Name a few, other than shredding," she said.

Well, how about pulling stuck cars out of mud holes?

She looked thoughtful. Then she said, "Let's see, we've had the place now for five years and no car has yet been stuck in the mud around here."

It could happen, I said.

"Besides," she argued, "you've got the truck. That was one of the reasons you gave for getting the truck, for pulling stuck cars out of mud."

Yeah, but what if the *truck* got stuck? Where would we be then?

"Good grief," she said.

Then I pointed out that for a few dollars extra you can get an attachment for the tractor that will enable you to pick up one of those big round bales of hay and carry it around behind you.

"Yeah, maybe Henry would let you borrow a bale of his hay," she said. Henry is one of our neighbors. He has cows and tractors and hay, all the proper things. "You could get out on the road with it. You could carry it all the way to Round Top and back, and wave at everybody."

I saw she was joking, but I sort of liked her idea of driving a tractor to town with a big round bale of hay on the back. I told her that sometimes it doesn't hurt to do certain things for the sake of appearance. For example, the little barn is not going to look right unless it has a tractor parked under its implement shed.

"What little barn?" she asked, and this time she wasn't joking.

I decided to back off, on the barn. I could see she's not quite ready for barns yet and I sort of wish I hadn't brought the matter up. I intended to get the tractor first and then introduce the need for a barn as a place to keep the tractor. Timing, man, timing. Remember your timing.

"Can you drive a tractor?" she asked, after I explained I was only kidding about the barn. (Ho ho ho. Just wait.)

Can I drive a tractor? You might as well ask if Michael Jordan can leap. Can Meryl Streep act? Can John Updike write? Honey, you are talking to one of the oldest living graduates of the Caprock Tractor Driving School, Class of '42. Back in those days . . . But never mind. Nobody wants to hear that old stuff.

In case you are wondering why I haven't bought the tractor, it's because the little sweetheart I want costs $8,500. And that's without the attachment that I don't need for carrying hay on the back.   ❧

Being Bill

Did I ever tell you that I used to be William Holden? I was, off and on, for something like thirty years, and it was a fine adventure.

I hadn't thought about this since back in the late seventies. Then the other day, I switched on the TV to check the weather and suddenly there I was on the screen, teaching Judy Holliday to talk properly in *Born Yesterday*.

So I forgot the weather. For half an hour, I watched that program, which was a kind of documentary about my career back when I was William Holden. It showed clips of some of my best pictures.

For a minute, I thought about trying to become him again, just one last time, but I decided against it. Because the guy is dead and—well, you can't be too careful these days.

You may think it's impossible for an ordinary person to become somebody else, but I did it without breaking a sweat. Did it in 1950 after I saw the film *Sunset Boulevard*. Why did I do it? Because I didn't much like who I was, or the way I looked, and I wasn't really in love then with what I did for a living. So I thought it would be nice to change and be somebody I liked better, at least on occasional weekends and holidays.

I picked Holden because, first, he looked the way I wanted

to look. He was moderately handsome but not pretty. His nose seemed kin to Bob Hope's, and sometimes when the camera caught him a certain way he looked really horse-faced.

But he also showed a kind of tragic, wounded face that appealed to women. And when he smiled, the smile was such a surprising contrast to his regular look that it made the receivers of it blink, and wonder, can this be the same face that was grieving just a minute ago?

Another thing was, Holden played the kind of parts I wanted to play, if I could have been a movie star.

With some exceptions. In fact, I didn't really enjoy playing opposite Gloria Swanson in *Sunset Boulevard*. Sure, that picture was my biggest break but Gloria Swanson, acting so silly and melodramatic, was no fun. Judy Holliday acting stupid was better.

You may recall that I got an Academy Award nomination for *Sunset Boulevard* and I did have great hopes. And then here came José Ferrer, collecting the Oscar for *Cyrano de Bergerac*. It wasn't easy, smiling through that evening, especially when Judy Holliday got best actress for *Born Yesterday* the same night.

Judy's a fine actress and all that, but I tell you one thing—she wouldn't even have gotten nominated if it hadn't been for me.

But that was okay, because I knew better things were coming, and they did. They came in '53, when I starred in *Stalag 17*. I got the Oscar for that one, and it was sweet, and I'll tell you why:

The competition was formidable. Guys like Marlon Brando, Montgomery Clift, Burt Lancaster, Richard Burton. They starred in big movies. *Julius Caesar. From Here to Eternity. The Robe.* And I won for *Stalag*. I was amazed. But my best and favorite role in all my career was in *The Bridge On The River*

Kwai, and I didn't get as much as a nomination for it from the Academy.

But never mind. On that TV show mentioned at the beginning, I got something better than an Oscar. Robert Mitchum, a friend of mine, told interviewers my performance in *River Kwai* was flawless. He indicated it was among the finest performances he has ever known.

That's remarkable because Mitchum doesn't go around distributing professional bouquets. He's pretty tough. Truth is, I was always a little afraid of him. Afraid he was about to explode at me, he's so gruff. Yet here he was giving me flowers. You can't ever tell about Mitchum.

You may wonder about Alec Guinness getting the Oscar for *Kwai* when I was so clearly the star. But in this business you learn to accept what's inevitable, and you stand in front of the TV cameras, smiling, and you say things like, "Alec is a consummate actor and certainly deserves the Academy Award." Even though you think you should have gotten it yourself.

Do you remember how tough I was in *The Wild Bunch?* Wow. I out-Johned John Wayne in that one. And then in *Network*, I moved from cowboy country to the board room without missing a beat.

Being William Holden was sure fun, and the only thing I didn't like about it was that you didn't recognize me. ❧

Sticks and Bones

One of my best friends weighs ninety pounds, and is still about five pounds overweight. She is a Labrador, the black kind, early middle age. Supposed to be a retriever.

She'll go fetch a stick if you throw it, but she won't bring it back. Instead she takes it off and chews it up and swallows it. A wood-eating dog.

She took a liking to sticks when she was a pup. I asked a vet about her habit of eating wood and he shrugged. Said she'd quit it when her puppyhood was over. That was five years ago.

This creature is purebred black Lab with a lot of championship kindogs. People who know Labs looked at her when she was a pup, lying over there swallowing sticks, and they'd say, "Pup like that ought to be trained. She'll be a happier dog, doing what she's bred to do." So we paid this trainer to come and teach her things. Sit. Stay. Heel. Down. Come front. All that stuff done by proper dogs.

She didn't much like being educated. When she saw the trainer coming to give another lesson she would run hide under the piano.

After each lesson, she seemed sadder instead of happier. I always felt sorry for her and would go outside and fetch her a fresh stick to eat.

When she was four and went to the vet for her checkup, we

told him she was still eating sticks and he said to get her one of those big old rawhide fake bones. "She won't eat that," he said.

She did, though. Hunkered down on the kitchen floor and chewed that thing up like it was a filet mignon and looked up and asked, "Is there another one?"

The people who give advice on what to feed dogs have gotten mighty restrictive, seems to me. Don't give 'em bones, they say. The mutts I knew in my early times didn't have champion foredogs like this Lab, but they stayed pretty healthy and what they ate was the same thing the hogs got—slop. And bones of all sorts.

When we had fried chicken for Sunday dinner, the women would say, "Now y'all save your bones for the dogs." I'm told now not to give the Lab a chicken bone because it might get hung in her throat or punch a hole in her insides and cause great trouble.

So I don't give her chicken bones, but if I did I think she'd chew 'em up like a potato chip. This is a dog that's consumed probably two hundred board feet of lumber since 1985. I bet those jaws would make powder out of a chicken leg bone.

The only food the Lab doesn't much like is her scientifically formulated, low-calorie-high-fiber dry pellets, prescribed for adult dogs with a weight problem. She'll eat it, but she'd rather have a banana, or a bowl of beans. I'm not sure I ought to tell you this, but last night I served her a green salad. I had salad left over, so I served her a bowl of it with vinegar and oil dressing, and she thought it was pretty nice. She prefers Roquefort dressing and so do I, but we can't have everything we want.

She likes all varieties of lettuce. Broccoli, too. Also spinach, cabbage, green beans, and Brussels sprouts.

We have a good time when we go to the country place.

(Think of all the sticks. Acres of them.) Early in the morning, we ride in the old truck. She loves that truck. We drive five miles into Round Top and get a *Chronicle* out of the rack in front of Klump's Grocery, and we eat little things we're not supposed to have. Tom's Toasted Peanuts. Lance's Cheese On Wheat. We mustn't do that, but we are without supervision so we do it anyway.

The Lab is proud of that truck. She doesn't understand that it's old, and rickety, and has 140,000 miles on it and might stop pretty soon and die on the road. She sits straight up, the way Labs can do, and her head is high as mine. Sometimes neighbors with dim sight or a quick look ask who that was, riding with me.

I say it was one of my good friends, who weighs about ninety and is five pounds overweight. ❧

Surprising Socks

Probably you have heard that washing machines will eat socks, but you may not believe it. I have run experiments relative to this matter and here's what I discovered:

A washer will, in fact, make socks disappear, just as you have heard. Furthermore, it can make missing socks reappear if it wants to. And a dryer can top a washer. A dryer can reproduce socks. I mean it can take a single sock and clone it and make a pair. I have proved these things.

I performed my socks experiments when I was left alone in the house and could do anything I took a notion to do, without interference. I selected six pairs of socks, all black and identical in size and shape. I placed them in the washer. Twelve black socks, in plain water. No soap.

While the socks went through fill, and wash, and rinse and spin dry, I sat in front of the washer the whole time and read a steamy paperback novel I bought at a book sale for fifty cents. The title of it is *Cast Off* and it's about this old boy who sets out to sail from San Francisco to Australia with an all-girl crew and the girls turn mean and mutiny and take over the vessel and put the guy ashore on an uncharted island in the South Pacific somewhere.

The book has nothing to do with the experiments. I mention it only to show that I stayed near the equipment and guarded it. Despite that no other person was in the house, I needed to be certain nobody messed with that washer while my tests were running.

At the end of spin dry, I took all the socks out and counted them and they totaled eleven. I examined the washer tub with a four-cell flashlight but found no sign of the twelfth sock and no clue as to what the washer did with it.

Since I had the time, and wanted to be thorough, I ran the socks through the cycle twice more. The second time another sock was missing. The third time—surprise. Both the missing socks reappeared.

My data on the washer seemed conclusive. A washer can take away socks, and it can restore them.

For years I have known about the taking away, and it was satisfying to obtain confirmation through a scientific experiment. The discovery that a washer is capable of returning socks it has taken—well, that was a bonus. Many significant developments in science come to us just that way, as happy spin-offs from research aimed at other targets.

I became interested in the field of sock washing during the eighties, when I was surviving a ten-year period as a bachelor and living in an apartment complex. I did my own laundry there, in coin-operated washers and dryers, and this was an adventure for me.

Automatic washing machines and I had not formed an acquaintance up to that time, and I was fascinated by the way a washer steals socks. The one I knew best preferred socks of color. At that time I was going through some mid-life changes and one of the symptoms was that I developed a liking for loud colors.

I bought bright socks, when all my previous life I'd worn only dark ones. I had yellow socks. Orange socks. Bright green ones. Fire truck red ones, which I actually wore in public. And the washing machines at that apartment ate them, fast as I could buy the things.

It was like paying a toll to wash socks, the way farmers took corn to the mill and the miller ground it and kept a part of the meal for payment. You put in six pairs of dirty socks and you got back five pairs of clean ones.

Except two of the pairs wouldn't be matched colors. Those apartment machines are the reason that all my socks today are black.

But I want to tell you about the most impressive result of my sock-washing research. Has to do with the dryer, not the washer.

I pitched six pairs of wet socks in the dryer, and when I fished them out I counted thirteen socks. This was exciting. Is it possible? Could the dryer be giving back to us the socks that the washer takes away?

I made a series of tests, and I am afraid to tell you the results because I think you wouldn't believe me. So I'm going to challenge you to do your own test. I doubt you'll do it but you might.

Put four wet socks in your dryer. Nothing else. Shut lid. Turn on dryer. Stay nearby. Do not leave while machine runs through cycle. When it shuts off, remove contents. Count the dry socks.

Be prepared for a surprise.

Sold on Staying Alive

$\mathcal{H}$e was looking good. All scrubbed and fresh and trimmed, as if he'd just come out of a barbershop. His clothes seemed new, and fit him well.

I checked his shoes when I got the chance. I always check shoes. They were close to perfect. If they were new as his shirt and suit, he must have had them worked over so they'd lose the too-new look that sharp dressers don't like.

But the greatest change was the life in his face, the light in his eye. He seemed interested in everything around us. Wanted to talk to strangers. When the waitress brought our coffee he told her she had beautiful hair, and her face lifted. He liked that, making a tired person smile.

He had called me to meet him for coffee, and to pay back some money he borrowed more than two years ago. Not a lot. In fact, I had written if off. But he hadn't. He gave it to me in new bills, so new they seemed powdery. Said he'd just been to the bank. It was pretty obvious something good had happened to this fellow.

Well, he was overdue for something good. I know that much.

Two years ago he was in the pits. Fifty-two and out of a job.

Worked for the same outfit more than twenty-five years and one day, pow, so long, Joe, we don't need you any more. That's pretty rough.

Some people can take a kick in the pants like that and cuss about it a little and get up off the turf and carry on. But not this guy. He was wounded.

"I'm afraid I ended up sort of enjoying it," he said, "in a kind of twisted way. I even quit shaving and taking a bath."

I remember the way he looked—really seedy—when he came around to borrow the money. He was leaning on friends then, getting fifty dollars here, seventy-five there. Grocery money.

"I went down really low," he said, talking about his bad time. That light in his eye faded. "Did you ever think seriously about doing yourself in? You know. Suicide?"

Me? Suicide? Naw.

"I came close," he said. "Little less than a year ago, between Thanksgiving and Christmas, that was when I was the lowest. I was driving toward town on Memorial one morning, and I had my shotgun in the car. Tell you the truth I was taking it to a friend's house, to sell. He'd offered me $100 for it.

"I got along there where the picnic grounds are and I thought, if he changes his mind and doesn't want the gun, I won't have enough gas to get back home. And I didn't have as much as a two-bit piece in my pocket.

"I turned in and pulled up to one of those picnic tables in the park and sat there and thought and that's when it hit me, about doing it. Solve all my troubles. I had the gun with me, and wasn't anybody else close around. That'd be good a place as any.

"Hard to believe now but for I guess ten minutes or more I fooled around there in the park, figuring out how to fix the gun in the front seat, so I could reach the trigger and do a neat job of it . . . ."

He stopped then, and a sort of dry chuckle came up from low in his throat. I asked why he didn't go ahead and do it.

"You won't believe why," he said.

Told him to try me anyhow.

"I didn't have any ammo," he said. "I had half a box of shells at home and I intended to bring them and give them to the guy that wanted the gun, and I drove off and forgot them.

"When I realized what I'd done it began to get so ridiculous, it was funny. I mean here's this guy who's so broke, and so mistreated, and he's suffered such a terrible injustice, and he's feeling so sorry for himself, he decides what the hell, he'll just commit suicide. And he pulls off the road and gets out his gun, and he hasn't got any ammo.

"I think probably I cried, at first, and then I'd laugh, and then cry some more, and laugh again, and when I got through, some way I was feeling better. I went on and took the gun and sold it and the next morning I cleaned up and went out looking for a job.

"Found one, too. It wasn't much, but inside of two months I got a better one, and I discovered something."

What was the discovery?

"I can sell," he said, and his tone was triumphant. "I'm a helluva salesman. I didn't know it. I just never had tried. I was always one of these guys who said he couldn't sell snow in the desert, but I think now I can sell anything people need, and it's fun, too."

When I watched him go, it hit me I hadn't asked him what he was selling, but judging from what he drove away in, I think it's cars.

This city has a multitude of stories, and sometimes they have happy endings.   ❧

She Put What?

Politicians we send to Washington from this state have been disappointing me one way or another for fifty years but this time my personal feelings have been wounded by Senator Kay Bailey Hutchison.

What the Senator has done, she entered a chili cook-off, representing our state, and you know what she put in her chili? Green bell peppers. *Bell Peppers.*

Senator, Senator, say it ain't so.

But even that felonious ingredient is not the worst stuff that went into the senator's chili. She also put in a large can of kidney beans.

That saddens me.

I don't have any trouble with beans in Texas chili but they ought not to be cooked together. Beans need to be an additive. Cooking beans in the same pot with the chili is pretty awful but if a Texan is really going to do that, at least she ought to use proper beans.

Pintos, that is. Certainly not kidney beans. I find the very term offensive. Please, don't talk to me about kidneys when we're making a delicate dish like chili.

By this time you're thinking that not even a politician can louse up Texas chili any worse than putting green bell peppers and kidney beans in it. Well, you're wrong. Get a good grip because here comes the final transgression. I hope you're ready:

Sen. Hutchison put into her chili four tablespoons of mole sauce.

A few among us may not know everything that goes into mole sauce. So hear this: One of the principal parts of that sauce is chocolate.

Chocolate? In Texas chili? I wonder why she didn't pitch in a few teaspoons of vanilla extract, and a cup or two of whipped cream.

I don't mind telling you I voted for Kay Bailey Hutchison. Helped send her to the U.S. Senate. And now she's gone up there and put chocolate in her chili.

Don't let me mislead you. I like green bell peppers, and red ones too, and yellow ones, and whatever other colors they come in. But bell peppers were put on this planet to be stuffed, or chopped up and pitched into a green salad. Kidney beans are all right, too, if you run out of pintos, but let's keep them in their proper place—not in the same pot with Texas chili. Even mole sauce is harmless if you're careful where you put it.

A few lines of type above, I said the worst news was that Sen. Hutchison's chili had chocolate in it. I take that back. Here's the worst news:

Her chili won the championship.

She was competing with other members of the Senate and the House of Representatives in an annual Congressional Club Chili Cook-Off. And she won, that's the bad thing.

It's bad because the whole world is now going to think that Texas chili has got green bell peppers in it, and kidney beans (I hate typing "kidney beans"), and that C-word.

Already I hear the argument that the senator didn't call her concoction Texas chili, as I've been referring to it. But that's no argument. Everything our U.S. senators do has the Texas brand on it, and here's the entire world reading that Mrs. Hutchison has won a chili-cookoff with a recipe that calls for bell peppers, kidney beans, and the C-word.

That damages the image of our state, and I cry out against it.

A couple of my advisers on national matters tell me that U.S. senators often are not really involved personally with things like recipes, which go forth under their names. They say senatorial staff members most often deal with such matters.

If that's true in this case, here's a piece of advice from one of Sen. Hutchison's constituents:

Get yourself a new cooking consultant. Because putting chocolate in chili cooked in Washington can cost you votes in Texas.

(Author's note: Sen. Hutchison accepted this criticism in good humor. She didn't promise to quit putting chocolate in her chili, but she did ask for my own favorite chili recipe to be included in a chili cookbook she was preparing. My favorite recipe is easy: Go to a grocery store, buy a package of Wick Fowler's Two-Alarm Chili Mix, and follow the directions.) ∾

He Wants to Hold the Check

*A*n insurance company I do a little business with has been trying to change my way of doing things. It wants to draft a monthly premium out of my bank account, and it's having a hard time understanding why I refuse to cooperate.

Between the first and the tenth day of every month, I write a check for the premium and send it to that company, and I have been doing that for years and years. The company tells me this is a cumbersome method of paying what I owe.

They tell me to imagine how much I have spent on postage over all the years. Think of the time I have invested, writing those checks and clipping the coupons and putting everything into envelopes and doing all that licking and sealing and going to the post office.

They point out that if I will simply sign the enclosed bank draft authorization, they will take my premium out of my account and I can forget about paying it. It'll be like I'm not paying.

What they don't understand is that I don't want to forget about paying. I want to remember, every month, that I am paying that insurance company those dollars. When I write their check I think about what I am getting for that money, and to wonder whether it is time to stop paying or keep on.

And don't worry about the trouble that going to the post office causes me. I like going to the post office and go every day, and sometimes twice. Right now if I went out and crawled in my pickup and cranked the engine I wouldn't even have to steer because that truck would go straight to the post office. It knows all the turns and where to park and how to get back.

Something else is that I'm not comfortable with strangers, in an insurance company or anywhere else, taking money out of my bank account. I don't need any help on that. I've always been able to take money out faster than I can put it in.

Other enterprises have also tried to get me to let them suck money out of the bank with that draft system. They tell me this is the future, in the matter of paying bills. They say everything is going to be electronic.

They say that eventually I won't need to write checks. They say that cash is going out of fashion, and that one day I'll carry a smart credit card and when I want anything I'll just flash that card and it will subtract dollars from my bank account.

No, thanks.

To show you what these folks are up against with old dudes like me, I don't even want strangers putting money *in* my bank account, much less taking it out.

Once a month, due to living as long as I have, I get a Social Security check. I don't apologize for this because I began contributing to Social Security in 1938 when I was riding a bicycle and delivering telegrams for Western Union back in my old hometown. And fifty years later I am still contributing so I figure it's about time to be getting something back.

The federal government is now trying to convince me I ought to let them send my Social Security payment electroni-cally. This means the government would punch buttons somewhere, and the buttons would credit my bank account with the money.

The government tells me that this electronic transfer system will protect me from mail theft. It says that thousands of government checks are stolen monthly before they reach where they are supposed to go.

It says that if I submit to electronic transfer I will no longer receive a check so I won't need to go to the bank to deposit it.

But I don't care anything about that. To begin with, I like going to the bank just as much as to the post office. And maybe more, because at the bank they serve free coffee and cookies in the lobby and sometimes I hear a good story or two.

Also I like getting the check, opening the envelope and seeing the amount and seeing my name on it and if I didn't get a check I wouldn't feel like I'd been paid.

I hate that government checks are being stolen, but from what I read in the papers the biggest thieves now are not stealing checks.

Instead they're punching buttons on computers somewhere to move money out of certain accounts and into others where it doesn't belong.

But it's not my money.

A Rumor on the Move

A fast-moving rumor flew around Houston last week, and it wasn't just a piece of routine gossip. It was of interest to a large number of citizens because I kept running into it almost everywhere I went.

I am not going to say here what the rumor was, or even hint in a general way what it was about, because I am still not certain whether there's an ounce of truth in it.

However, I confess an interest in rumors, although the information they carry is so often inaccurate. My main interest is in the way rumors travel, and how they get changed as they move along.

Long ago in my early times we played a parlor game that demonstrated the evolution of rumors in circulation. I don't recall the name of the game but the way we played, we'd get about twenty or twenty-five kids in a circle. A designated person would think up a short statement, write it on a slip of paper, put the slip under a hat, then whisper the words to the next person in the circle.

Then that person would whisper the words to the next person, and so on around the circle until the last person received the message, and spoke it aloud. And it was seldom the same message.

Generally it ended up twisted out of shape, and often it was funny, and caused everybody in the circle to whoop when the original statement was taken from under the hat and read. This was counted to be great entertainment, back when children were easier to entertain than now.

Sometimes, when the message was moving around the circle, somebody would change it on purpose, hoping to improve it, make it funnier or more interesting. That was against the rules, but it was consistent with the way rumors are mangled and aggravated in the adult world.

The rumor I kept hearing last week first crossed my trail in a post office parking lot on West Gray. It came in the form of a question, a popular way to move a rumor along. A gent asked me if I had heard that such and such a thing had happened. I had not, but the information was in my head then, and subject to additional circulation.

And I did move it along, on the telephone. I called a friend who is usually well-informed on matters of that sort. He said yes, he had heard the rumor but hadn't been able to establish whether there's any truth in it. Also he hadn't heard it quite the way I had, and he was interested in exactly what I had heard, and when, and from whom.

So I told him, and he said that was interesting, which I believe meant that what I had heard was maybe more spectacular than the version he had heard. When I hung up the phone it occurred to me that I had called to get information, and instead I had given some out, when I didn't intend to.

The next day I heard the rumor again in the parking lot of the Post Oak YMCA. Parking lots are somehow suited to the exchange of rumors.

The rumor at the Y included the information I had given my friend on the phone, plus a couple of new morsels which, if true, made the rumor even more interesting than when I got the first wind of it.

Then on Wednesday I got the rumor at the post office on Gray again, but by that time it had moved out of the parking lot and into the lobby where the mail boxes are, and it had matured. It had gained strength.

It had become a story with a solid shape. It had a beginning and a middle and an end and people whose names you would know were being quoted, saying this is all true. I almost began believing.

But on Wednesday, when the rumor glanced off me at the Exxon station on the corner of San Felipe and Weslayan, it had deteriorated.

It was out of control by then. It was showing way too many options. You could pick over it and choose any of three or four versions and take the one you preferred. It was like kids had gotten control of it, and were playing that old rumor game where we sat in a circle and whispered little lies to one another.

When a rumor gets in that condition, it loses its punch and dies. This happens often. A rumor is planted that way, and sprouts and shows great promise, and it gets fertilized and cultivated, but it grows out of control and falls over.

By Thursday afternoon, outside the *Chronicle* building at the corner of Milam and Prairie, I was hearing that there's no truth in that rumor. But I'm still not certain.

(Author's note: The rumor this piece refers to was that the Belo Corporation had purchased the Houston Post, *the* Chronicle's *principal competition. This was of interest to me because Belo is the parent of the* Dallas News *and if the report had been true, the lives of all* Chronicle *staff members might have changed significantly. But the* Post *not long afterward went out of business, so the rumor was false.)* ∾

Buddy's Back

*S*he stopped me on the sidewalk in front of the drugstore and asked, "Would you like to hear a sad story?"

Asking me if I want to hear a story, sad or happy, is about the same as asking a drunk if he wants a beer. I told her to go ahead and this is the story she told:

"In 1972, my younger brother ran away from home. He was fifteen. My mother always said she thought the Gypsies stole him. The old people in her family believed that kind of thing, that Gypsies would steal children.

"My Dad used to tell Mama that if the Gypsies or anybody else stole Buddy they'd bring him home before dark and pay you to take him back. Dad and Buddy had a hard time getting along. They were always on one another's case. Too much alike, I guess.

"Buddy wasn't the kind of bad kid that went around robbing drive-in grocery stores, but some way or other he had trouble fitting into the world. He never did make any real friends, and he wouldn't study, and he was always cutting out of school. He'd take things, like at home, and if you caught him he'd say he was just borrowing. I used to catch him taking money out of my purse and he'd say, 'Well, come on, Grace, gimme a break, I'm just borrowin' a couple of bucks, Okay?' Of course he'd never pay it back.

"What Buddy was good at was lying. He was a world class liar. He could look you straight in the eye and tell you the house was on fire and make you want to believe it, even when you knew it wasn't the truth.

"My Dad spent two years looking for that kid. He'd call Buddy good riddance and then get on an airplane and fly all the way to Chicago or somewhere to follow up some vague clue he'd gotten hold of. In '74, Dad found Buddy's grave, up in Missouri. The county up there had buried him. His name on the records was wrong, but one thing was right. The records described the body and said it had an oval birthmark on the inside of the left thigh. Buddy had that. It was a dark brown birthmark shaped like a football. When he was a little boy that's what he called it, his football. Anyhow, we said it was Buddy, and laid him to rest.

"Okay, then last spring, on the tenth day of June, this person showed up on my door step. He said, 'Grace? Don't you know me? It's Buddy. It's me.'

"I didn't believe it. He didn't look like Buddy. He was fat, for one thing. I mean the kind of fat where his neck pooched out over his collar, you know? Buddy was always skinny as a snake. And his color looked different. Too dark. Buddy was light-skinned.

"But he knew things Buddy would know. He knew my birthday. He knew about Buster, our old dog. Knew enough that I let him in. Something about his eyes was Buddy. We sat in my living room two hours and I tried to cross him up, prove to myself he wasn't Buddy. But I *wanted* him to be Buddy. I'm pretty well alone. Dad's dead. Mama's in a nursing home. I'm divorced. I can use a brother, right?

"I told him, 'There's one thing you could show me to prove you're Buddy.' He grinned and said, 'You mean my football.'

He pulled his pants leg up and showed me the birthmark, and that did it.

"For a month, I felt like I was born again, having my brother back. And he was changed. He was so sweet and good. He cleaned house. He cooked for me. Mowed the lawn. Fixed things around the place that hadn't been fixed since my husband left. And he was good to Mama. He'd go to see her every day, do for her.

"He told me, 'Grace, I'm down on my luck just now but I'm trying to get my life back together.' I gave him money. Keys. My God, I even gave him a checkbook. I needed a brother so bad.

"I guess I don't have to tell you he disappeared again, exactly a month after he came. Sure, he cleaned me out. Left me ten bucks in the bank. I wonder why he left that much. He took my car, and almost everything in the house he could convert to cash. Silver. Jewelry. Appliances. They found the car up on Interstate 45 but it was stripped. You won't believe this. He took Mama's diamond ring off her finger, while she was asleep in the nursing home. What do you think of all that?"

I told her these con men are sharp. They find things out, even about dead people, even about things like birthmarks, and the names of good old dogs.

She said, "Oh, this wasn't anybody pretending. This was my brother, all right, and the sad thing is that I still love him."   ❧

High Water Flowers

"Talking about your wildflowers, you can't ever tell what you'll get in the way of blossoms in a spring wet as this. You may get strange ones, flowers you haven't ever seen before, and might not see again for thirty years."

That short speech came out of Madame Z, my Brazos Bottom fortune-teller friend, who made it while leaning on a broom. We were standing at the gate in her front yard, having our March visit. Facing west, looking toward the grove of native pecans that stands at the foot of the slope that marks the edge of the river bottom.

Reason for the broom, Madame was sweeping her front yard.

Some city dwellers may find it strange that a person would go out and sweep a yard. But a multitude of white-haired country folks will count it perfectly normal.

Madame's yard is hard-packed red clay and sand, and has never been sodded or seeded to make a lawn. Most country yards in this state were like that in my early times, and you swept them the same as you swept the house. People didn't want grass in their yards. Not having grass in the yard was what made it a yard, distinguished from a pasture where the cows were.

There at the gate Madame and I talked about all the rain

we've had, and the river rises, and the effect of such events on animals and trees and bushes and flowers.

"High rises on the river," she said, "that's what created this wide bottom to begin with, and made it a special place to grow things. In these fields around here I expect you could dig down fifty feet or more and still find rich dirt, and it doesn't even belong here. It washed down on rises, from way up the river, from no telling how far, and settled here when the overflow went down."

Madame flicked her broom at a scattering of twigs. What you do when sweeping a yard is push the leaves and sticks into piles, and pick them up, and fling them over the fence.

"Seed comes down on those rises, too," Madame went on. "All kinds of seed, and a lot of it is strange to this part of the country. Sometimes in spring it sprouts, or tries to, and tests out the climate to see if it feels like home.

"When I was a girl I was working upriver a good way, and one spring there was a big rise and when the river went back in its banks, all our low places in the bottom sprouted a ferny kind of a flower with the prettiest blossom, some pink and some purple.

"We never had seen flowers anything like that," Madame said. "We'd gather them up by the armful, and bring them in, and they were so pretty. We called them ditch roses, because they wouldn't grow anywhere except in low places. Most of your wildflowers enjoy high places that drain off, but these wanted wet dirt, and they'd pass on away when the ditches dried out.

"And smell good? Lordy. I'm telling you, those little roses smelled sweet as sugar. You could walk along a turnrow in a field and take a breath and it was like drawing in drugstore perfume.

"Honeybees came in here to the river bottom like we never

saw. Bumblebees, too. And hummingbirds? I hadn't ever seen a hummingbird in this bottom until that year the ditch roses bloomed, and those little dickens were everywhere, zipping and chirking and cluttering their wings. Beat anything I ever saw.

"People loved those flowers. And bees made the best honey that spring. Ditch rose honey got famous, all up and down the river. I bet if I had me a jar of ditch rose honey right now I could peddle it for big money."

Madame paused, and reached out with her broom and drew a little trash to the pile at her feet. I asked if she could show me any of those ditch roses that might be blooming now.

She shook her head. "No, I sure can't, because I've never seen one of those bushes again. The seed must have floated in on the river rise, and came up, and bloomed that one year."

A sluggish red wasp made a pass at us and Madame took a swing at it with her broom. "What I think," she said, "is the seed from all those ditch roses is still in the ground in this bottom, and one of these times when things get just right, they'll sprout and bloom again.

"Why don't you bring the other broom out of the kitchen, and let's get this yard swept?" ∾

He Has a Record

A group of friends came to me recently with what they called a feeler. They wanted to know how I would feel about running for public office.

I am not going to say which office. I had to refuse the offer and the friends asked me to keep quiet about it because they didn't want the next person they asked to know he was second choice. (I have since made sly inquiries and found out I was the fourth choice myself, but never mind.)

It is, of course, an honor to be asked to run for office, and I grieve that my past is too shady to stand up under the scrutiny I would get from the media during a political campaign. The thing that would come out, oh my. I would be an embarrassment to my party and my family and my country. I will tell you why, if you won't spread the word around.

In 1937 I was charged and convicted of making an inappropriate sexual advance to Bettye Earle Henderson in a darkened movie theater. There, I have told it. This is on my record, and there is nothing I can do now to change it.

Bettye Earle was one of the prettiest girls in our school, back in my old hometown. Her mother and mine were pillars in the Women's Missionary Society. Bettye Earle played the violin. She sang in the choir. She made all A's in school. Bettye Earle Henderson was a very nice girl.

Along about this time I had noticed that a good many of the guys and girls in my class had started walking around holding hands, and in public places, at that. Even in the halls at school.

I had not done any handholding but I could see that it was an exciting activity and I longed to give it a try. The hand I wanted to hold belonged to Bettye Earle Henderson.

By talking to some of the more experienced guys I learned that you didn't just walk up and grab a girl's hand and hold it. There were preliminaries. You talked, first. You talked about the weather, and about what you did last summer, and whether you were going to take solid geometry. You bought them a Nehi soda water. You took them to the picture show. Then maybe you could work around to handholding.

I was able to see the importance of girls but I wasn't yet qualified to talk to them. I needed practice. So I practiced by talking to cows.

Before and after school then I was milking a couple of cows, and delivering the milk to various customers around town, and I kept inviting the cows to go to the picture show with me until at last I was fairly comfortable with the routine. One day at school my courage rose up inside me and I asked Bettye Earle to go to the picture show and she said yes.

We went on a Saturday afternoon, because I knew better than to ask her to go anywhere after dark.

Walking to the show, we got the necessary talking done. We agreed that the weather was cold. The previous summer she had been to Galveston with her parents and she talked about the waves, and the shells she picked up, and she asked if I knew about undertow. I had never seen salt water then and wouldn't until I was twenty-two years old so I didn't know about undertow. But neither of us intended to take solid geometry so I supposed I was doing fine—common ground established on two out of three tries.

The picture show was a splendid production, with six-shooters firing forty-eight times without reloading, and stage-coaches getting robbed left and right, and toward the middle of the show I made my move.

I reached for Bettye Earle's hand and somehow in the dark and in the excitement my reach was misdirected and my hand landed by accident on her knee. On the knee, of Bettye Earle Henderson.

She gasped and rose out of her seat in a leap. She left the theater. She went home. She told her mother. Her mother told mine. Before I got home I was convicted.

Charged, tried and pronounced guilty by Bettye Earle's mother and mine—two jurists who made up the highest court in the land.

The families had a conference and decided to keep the matter under wraps, so that my reputation and my life would not be forever ruined, and I would not have to leave town. But it was decreed that I was never again to go near enough to Bettye Earle Henderson to touch her. And I did not.

More of this story is true than you probably think.　　∽

A Sporting Forecast

My friend Mel was lying back in the soft red chair here in the office, reading the paper and commenting on the news. "If our football team really moves to Tennessee just because we won't build them a bigger stadium," he said, "they're fools. They don't need a bigger stadium. In another few years we'll be using big stadiums as warehouses."

Oh? How does he figure that?

"Because all the spectators at sporting events are gonna be sitting at home in front of their TV sets," Mel said, raising his arms in resignation, as if everybody ought to see that what he says is so. "The Astrodome is already too big. In another ten years, maybe sooner, the Oilers could be playing in any high school stadium in Harris Country and making Bud Adams richer by the week."

Was he talking about pay TV?

"Of course. It's the only possible answer for spectator sports. It makes no sense to invest millions of dollars in a sports team, and a huge stadium, and then depend on fans showing up and paying to get in. Ask that baseball fellow who owns the Astros. McBain?"

McLane. But how do you know fans would pay to watch a game on television?

He raised his arms again. "Because it's so much easier. And

cheaper, man. Say you're a family of four, and you love base-ball. You go out there to the Astrodome and park and buy hot dogs and pop and a couple of beers, you've ruptured a fifty dollar bill, at least, and probably more. How many times a year are you going to do that?"

But what would a family like that pay to watch a baseball game on TV?

"If they paid as much as ten bucks they'd save a ton," Mel said. "They're sitting at home watching that Bagman guy hit home runs and they're eating homemade hamburgers and if the game gets slow they can go on to bed without fighting traffic for an hour."

Bagwell, I said, not Bagman. But how about the excitement of being in the stadium, in the crowd, close to the action? Hard-core fans always say nothing compares to being there.

"That's getting ready to change," Mel said. "Haven't they heard about virtual reality? Listen, man, television is on the brink of a huge revolution. Pretty soon, a fan watching TV at home is going to be closer to the action than he'd be if he was sitting in the best seat in the house. He won't just see Baggio playing second base, he'll be out there with him, standing beside him."

Biggio, I said, not Baggio.

"Whatever," Mel said, waving me off. "In basketball? It'll be fantastic. When Malloy (I think he meant Maloney) dribbles the ball down the court, going in for two, the TV fan will be running with him, right out there in the middle of the floor. Listen, sports on TV will be so real, so good, that nobody will buy a ticket to attend a game because it'll be so much better on TV."

Assuming that comes to pass, it still sounds mighty expen-sive.

"But it's not," Mel said, and pointed to my TV over in the

corner. "You have cable here. When you want a movie, you pick up the phone, dial the number on the screen, and here comes the film and the charge goes on your bill. How much? Do you know?"

Around four bucks, I think.

"Which is about half what you'd pay to see a movie at a theater," Mel said. "And your wife is watching, too, and maybe a couple of visitors. This shows you what's gonna happen to movie theaters. They'll be in the same boat with sports stadiums, and sinking."

But these cable movies aren't first-run films.

"No," Mel said, "but they will be, don't worry. It's just flat inevitable."

At any rate, getting back to the Oilers, looks like they're already gone to Nashville so we can stop worrying about watching them.

He was shaking his head. "I'm not convinced they're gone. It would be so easy to keep them."

Easy? How so?

"You simply form a corporation," Mel said, his arms raised again, "sell stock to the public, and buy the team from Adams. Let 'em play in the Astrodome a few more seasons, until we don't need it any longer. I'll bet you we've got millions of people who'd like to own a few shares in a pro football team. Wouldn't you?"

Let me think. I might, at that.

Saving Ray from Maggie

*L*ately for purposes of entertainment I've been reading the *Chronicle Connection* ads in the paper on Fridays. You haven't missed them, have you? Entire pages of classified-type advertisements bought by people searching for new friends. Most seem to be looking for romance.

These kinds of ads interest me because they can change lives, and I believe it's a mistake not to take them seriously. I found this out a long time ago, when I was in high school and my mother was running a boardinghouse back in our old hometown.

We called that place a boardinghouse even though in addition to serving meals we rented rooms and the roomers and boarders were almost the same as family. Some we'd keep up with, years and years after they moved on.

One I think of when I read the *Chronicle Connection* ads was Ray W., a quiet and polite bachelor of maybe forty, and so shy he seemed to suffer active pain from it. My father used to say Ray was so timid you couldn't ask him to pass the butter without making him blush.

Ray was tall and slender and bookish. Wore dark horn-rims. We always said he looked like Harold Lloyd, which won't mean much to anybody younger than sixty. Harold Lloyd was an actor who — well, who looked like Ray W., tall and slender and bookish and wore dark horn-rims.

Ray kept himself shut away in his room most of the time. I used to wonder what he did in there, for hours at a stretch. Finally we found out one thing he did was write letters to this woman, this sort of pen pal. He'd made contact with her through what we then called a lonely hearts magazine. I'm thinking now Ray must have rented a post office box for this purpose, because I sneaked a look at all mail that came to that big house and none of it was ever addressed to Ray.

The first we knew about this was when Ray went to my mother, so worried he had fever, and told her Maggie was coming.

My mother grilled the facts from Ray concerning this Maggie woman. What kind of letters had Ray been writing to her?

He said just friendly letters.

They weren't love letters?

Ray said no, at least not exactly.

What did that mean, not exactly? Did he write Maggie that he loved her?

Ray said yes but he didn't mean it the way it sounded. He was lonesome and he liked the letters and he liked writing to Maggie about romance, and houses, and children, but he didn't intend for her to take him so seriously.

Why was Maggie coming?

Well, Ray said, because she thought Ray was going to marry her.

And did he ask her to marry him in one of the letters?

Ray said no. Then he said he didn't know, for sure. He said he couldn't remember. He said he might have but he didn't mean to. He begged my mother to help him, and went back upstairs to his room and stayed.

Word got around, you might say, about this adventure. The first we knew Maggie really was coming, one of my mother's Missionary Society ladies, who lived back toward town, said a red-headed woman carrying a blue suitcase was walking our way and she bet it was Maggie herself. And it was.

Everybody at home took over windows as observation posts, to get an advance look at Maggie. I hid in the high shrubbery in front of the house. I thought she looked pretty nice. Good sturdy person. Carried that big suitcase like it was empty. I knew my mother would figure she'd used too much powder and paint, and I'd have bet you a big red barn she dyed her hair.

My mother took Maggie in her sewing room and kept her in there talking more than two hours, explaining the best she could about Ray, and all the time that woman was in the house Ray came never down to meet her or even stuck his head out of his room. In fact, he didn't come down to supper that night, after Maggie left. I remember taking soup up to him. It was like he'd been scared into being some kind of invalid.

Maybe you're saying this was a pretty wicked stunt to pull on Maggie.

But I'm not sure. The story we've told and retold all these years is that Maggie did not go back to where she came from, that she stayed right there in the old hometown, got a job waiting tables at the Deluxe Cafe, married a truck driver off Highway 80 and moved to Abilene. ❧

The First Jacket Morning

For several days here at the old country house in Washington County we've been feeling the early signs of fall, but it seemed ridiculous to mention them when the thermometer on the front porch was still climbing to the nineties in the afternoons.

But the promises of fall have little to do with temperature. I see it first in the quality of light. Shadows grow longer, and the light softens and seems to show a pale orange tint.

Leaves on the post oaks and black jacks haven't begun to drop yet but they're through doing their work and they've become papery and they've shrunk a little.

Out in the scrub timber west of the house there's an old cottonwood that announces the end of summer with the dry clutter of its leaves. The tree is maybe a hundred yards from this front porch and I've been hearing the sound of its leaves off and on since the middle of August, but not before then.

The hummingbirds have been passing through the past few days, too, on their way to wherever hummingbirds go in winter. They don't stay with us long.

Also the grasshoppers are fading. They've still got a lot of fading to do but at least now you can walk through the grass without getting hit in the mouth by one of the things. The hoppers had a really successful summer here on this reservation, the best in years, and I think they're why the hummingbirds don't stick around. Hoppers have chewed up most of the flowers that make blooms hummingbirds like. The blooms we have left now are mostly antique roses and hummingbirds don't care for them. They'll pause at a rose, and hover, and consider. Then zip away without a taste.

My guess is, the reason for all the grasshoppers is that we've used that Logic material here in the yard for two years and we've got the fire ants pretty well controlled. Then came grasshoppers, a very plague of them, soon as the ants were thinned out. Which is the trouble with poisoning. You get rid of one plague and another arrives to take over. It almost comes down to which plague you'd rather live with.

Over the past week the cicadas have just about stopped buzzing. Another sign of dying summer.

Acorns have begun to fall and hit the tin roof with a metallic bang.

Then you have the more subtle hints. Watch the old dog. She'll sense a change far earlier than we do. She'll raise her head from a nap as if she's been called, when no one has called her. She'll go out in the side yard and point herself north and raise her nose and half-close her eyes and stand there a full minute, reading the air, finding things out, things that are far away and won't happen for days.

Faint telling odors come over the land, too. The smell of curing grass and drying leaves. Blind people know this sign. I had a blind neighbor once and she was the best foreteller of Earth events I've known.

I'm doing this report on Labor Day, and the signs suddenly are not so vague.

We had a nice little push of cool air come through during

the night and at eight o'clock I needed a jacket to sit outside. The first jacket morning. The jacket didn't last long. It's eleven a.m. now and the temp about eighty-three and may go to ninety-odd but that doesn't matter. For me, summer is over when we've had our first jacket morning.

Everything considered, it's been a pretty fair season. June and July were dry but in August we measured seven inches in the front fence rain gauge. Our live oaks grew and stayed healthy.

Those trees are by far the most significant feature of this small patch of woods. The house and other improvements are nothing, against these trees. They make the place worth having, worth spending what we spend on it. Inside the yard fence are five large live oaks nicely spaced from one another and we call them old. They are not old. They're in their prime, and could live for hundreds of years, and in some future century make this acreage truly special.

I don't really grieve much when the grasshoppers eat the flowers. What I worry about is the tree disease that has killed so many of this state's live oaks. I have friends who have sat on country porches like this and watched their live oaks die and I would endure that at a considerable price.

We inspect these oaks daily for symptoms, like parents guarding the health of their children. When September comes and the oaks are happy, it's been a good summer.   ∾

Remembering Scotland

*H*ere's my theory on foreign travel for pleasure: When you go across oceans to faraway places, the principal reward doesn't even begin until about a year after you get home.

When you're on the journey you're not really your normal self, unless you're what they call a seasoned world traveler, and most of us aren't. You may be tired or half sick when you depart, because of the mighty effort required to get ready. Then when you're in exotic places seeing special sights and having new experiences, how can you be in a relaxed and thoughtful state?

More likely you're on some kind of strange high, a combination of excitement and confusion. Existing in an odd culture. Dealing with money exchange, mix-ups in schedules, anger over what you perceive as mistreatment by taxi drivers or airline clerks. But you plow ahead, and take your pictures, and come back home telling anybody who'll listen how wonderful it was. When maybe the truth is you're relieved to get back to the office or the kitchen.

My experience has been that time will filter out the negatives, and months later on a quiet evening at home you can look at all the pictures again, and begin enjoying your travels.

I'm thinking now about a trip my partner and I took to

Scotland several years ago. I'm sure it wasn't a perfect trip but now it is, in memory, and we have taken it again many times.

We go back to see if Mr. Stewart is still there, in the ancient hotel at Torridon in the Northwest Highlands. This is not a small hotel but Mr. Stewart seemed to operate it all by himself. He met us out front when we drove up in the little rent car. He was behind the desk when we registered. He carried our bags upstairs.

When we had questions about the area, Mr. Stewart came out to answer. Guess who brought up the extra pillow we asked for. The next morning, guess who helped me rig the fly rod I rented back in Inverness, loaned us a couple of flies, and showed us where to fish. When we were on that rugged mountain stream and a cold rain came to sting and chill us, guess who showed up on the mountainside and brought us raincoats.

So it got to be a pleasant joke. We'd say, "Don't worry, if we fall on these rocks and break a leg, Mr. Stewart will come and set it."

I'm afraid we laughed, and a bit too loud, the first time we ate in the hotel dining room and the waiter who served our food was Mr. Stewart. But he understood our laughter and forgave us.

At that dinner he served us sea trout. We asked if the fish were local and he said yes, that he had caught them out of Lake Torridon the night before.

When we drove away from that place Mr. Stewart was standing out front, waving goodbye, and we thought it almost mysterious that he appeared so healthy, this slender Scot who operated a one-man hotel all day and fished for trout at night.

Here is one of the photos from that same trip. It shows the lonely house on the moor, with the sheep at the front door. I keep this picture out and study it frequently because I have the haunting notion that I once lived there.

In a previous life? Who knows? Maybe so.

The day we saw the house we had been in the Highlands about a week and roamed through its smooth treeless mountains and along the shores of those mystical lakes and every day the feeling that I had been there before kept getting stronger. We laughed about it a little. I told my partner I was probably just recalling pictures in geography books I had seen long ago in school.

One afternoon we drove the rent car several miles up a narrow road that runs along one of those dark lakes. Lonely country. We met no cars. Saw no people. Clouds were low and thick. The light so weak the green mountains turned close to black.

We went round a bend and saw a house ahead. Nobody was in the house, or near it. There were no outbuildings. No human clutter. Just two sheep standing at the front door. The peculiar thing is, I was not surprised by sheep at that door. It was as if I knew the house, knew in advance the sheep would be there.

We stopped and I got out to take this picture I keep. The house is a single rectangle with a high gable roof. Two dormers rise out of the roof on each side of the front entrance. The building stands so close to the road you could pull up in front, take one step and be inside the door, and that didn't seem wrong to me. It seemed familiar, in fact.

I almost said aloud, but I didn't because I was afraid my partner would think I had gone funny in the head, "You see that extension of the main house, on its left end, with the rock walls? That was used as a shelter for sheep in cold weather. I can remember herding sheep through that door. And I have slept in the upstairs room behind those dormers, and looked out at the mist on the lake at sunrise."

I confess I was uncomfortable there. But my partner loved the lake and its shore. Called it enchanting, and got out and walked on the slopes and liked the feel of the wind and the softness of the ground. The surface in that part of the world is often spongy because of the peat that covers it and on that day the softness suggested instability to me, as if the ground might give way and cave in and I didn't much like walking on it.

So I was relieved to be gone from there. But, now, time has wiped away that discomfort and I would love to go back, and stay a while, and see what I might feel on a second visit. I've decided this: If it's true that people have previous lives, and if I had any, one of them I spent as a sheepherder on that lonely lake in Scotland.

Another small gem of a happening occurred on the splendid fast train we took, from London up to Edinburgh. We sat facing a middle-aged red-faced Scot who was going home to Aberdeen, and he had his elderly mother with him.

We are shameless rubbernecking tourists. We look out windows all the time for things we've never seen before. From that train we kept seeing pretty lavender flowers, miles and miles of these blossoms along the railroad. We asked the Scot across from us, "What flower is this?"

He watched out the window for a while. Then nudged his mother and spoke to her quietly. She lifted herself and watched for maybe half a mile, and the two then conferred with serious faces. At last the son announced, "It's waild."

Ah, yes. Waild. What a fine name for a flowering plant in rural Britain. We wondered for several miles if we might collect seed from those Waild plants, and take them home.

Then it struck us, after listening to a few more remarks from

Scottish passengers, that the man was not telling us the name of the plant, but simply that it was wild. It was a *waild*flower.

This term now occupies an honorable position in private dialect around our premises. We no longer have anything wild. It's all waild, instead. Waildlife. Waildcat. Waildfire. What kind of flower is that? It's waild.

The very sound of that word is an entertainment to me but the best thing about it is, it brings back the image of those earnest red faces, frowning in concentration, trying to answer a request from a couple of American tourists. ❧

There Were Children Here

*T*his is as nice an afternoon as we've seen in almost six weeks in Europe. It's like a Texas spring day that we brag about. Air is fresh and sweet to breathe, warm in direct sun, cool in the shade. A sweater feels comfortable here in the shadows.

I've found a bench in a patch of woods. A weeping willow is beside the bench. I can almost lean against a great conifer and behind it various kinds of hardwoods are throwing most of this shade. I have not learned the name of trees over here very well, or birds. Some sort of little warblers are singing overhead.

As nice a day as this is, still I am surprised that birds sing here.

In front of my bench is a broad open space covered in white gravel and it is like a schoolyard to me. Maybe that's because of the building I face. It has an institutional appearance. I have seen elementary schools back home built very much like it.

Well, there were children here, all right.

The outside walls are yellow-orange brick. Windows and doors are painted pale green. The roof is a dark brown tile.

The building is about two hundred feet long and narrow, only one room deep. Built in 1942.

One feature is not consistent with schoolhouses. No small school would need the massive brick chimney rising from the center of the roof. This chimney served the four brick ovens in the middle sections, where the bodies were burned.

The ovens are still in there and they look a lot the same as ovens I have seen in commercial bakeries.

This building here inside the barbed wire fences of Dachau Concentration Camp also has one of those famous Nazi "shower rooms" with the nozzles rigged to spew poison gas and kill an entire roomful of Jews all at once. But the record says the gas chamber was never used. They didn't gas them at Dachau. They hanged them, or shot them or tortured them to death or let them die of disease or starvation, or suicide.

There was an easy way to commit suicide. A concrete ditch runs all around the camp—just inside the barbed wire fences, which have at least a dozen strands plus entanglements at the bottom. And beside the ditch is a strip of short-mowed grass about twenty-five feet wide. All a prisoner had to do was take one step onto that grass strip and he would be shot immediately from a guard tower.

In the room where the ovens are, heavy wooden timbers support the roof and many of the prisoners were hanged from those timbers before they were cremated. Others died by "hanging at stake." I was not familiar with this method of killing people, but I went through the museum here and saw photos of how it was done. The procedure required the victim to be suspended by the neck from a rope attached to the top of a single sturdy post about eight feet tall. Seeing those photos suggested crucifixion to me.

Off to my left maybe a quarter of a mile is the "firing range" of the SS troops. It was really an execution range. Just stand them up there and mow them down, by the hundreds. It is not known how many died in this awful place. Thousands, yes. At least 31,000 for sure, because they were registered. Many other victims were not.

A short drive to the south lies the beautiful little city of Dachau. It's more than 1,200 years old and was once known as a mecca for European artists, an art colony. I feel a tug of pain for that town, because who thinks of a city when they hear the name Dachau? More likely they hear the name as a synonym for Nazi horror. This was the first concentration camp built, in 1933, to implement Hitler's plan to exterminate the Jews, and all his political enemies. Not all those who were imprisoned or died at Dachau were Jews.

The record of Nazi atrocities survives here, inside these fences, documented with chilling photographs. The record is preserved by the state of Bavaria and an organization called the Dachau International Committee. One of the original barracks stands, and the concrete foundations of all the others lie in correct rows on white gravel and they made me think of a military cemetery.

I stood among them and tried to feel what I thought I ought to feel, here where the most terrible things that humans ever did to other humans were done, and done in my lifetime. I could see these things going on. The suffering and the death. And some of it seemed to be spiritual torture, administered purely for the sake of evil—forcing prisoners, for instance, to march and play band instruments and lead a parade of friends on the way to their execution.

But on this bench in the shade, on such a pretty day, and with the birds singing, what I feel is that this is the saddest place I ever was, here at a crematorium which looks so much like a school where little children could learn to read and to love one another. ✥

*I*n late February of 1978 Old Friend Morgan and I were sharing a toddy and taking inventory of our lives. The day was cold and the cold penetrated our bones and made us feel old. We longed for spring, and a fresh beginning.

We thought dark thoughts. "What if we died," said O.F., "and never saw another spring?"

We poured another toddy to dispel the gloom and soon afterward came to a decision: We should go look for spring, to find it and dwell in it a while, to make certain we would experience at least one more time spring's spiritual renewal. The first week of March we loaded up and headed south from Houston.

"Where are you going?" friends asked.

"We're going to find spring," we said.

"But how will you know when you find it?" they wondered.

A fair question. Early in March, common signs of spring usually occur not more than a day's drive down the coast from Houston, but they aren't dependable. The temperature can climb to ninety and grass will turn green and bluebonnets will be six inches tall and the buds of foolish trees will burst and put forth tender foliage. Then, often as not, here will come a whistling norther and the mercury will sink into the twenties and put three-quarters of the state right back into winter. Going south in Texas to find spring is not as simple as it sounds.

We needed a dependable spring indicator, and we chose mesquite trees.

O.F. and I both grew up in mesquite country where our forebears depended on mesquites to announce the arrival of spring. Those good folks could be standing ankle deep in green grass, breathing the fragrance of blooming wildflowers, but they refused to believe they were safe from a killing frost unless mesquites had leafed out. O.F. and I were baptized in the belief that mesquites know more about the seasons than the National Weather Service, all the television meteorologists combined, or any wild goose.

That first year the mesquites found spring for us near the city of Falfurrias, not far off the twenty-seventh parallel of latitude. We reported this in the column, felt better for having confirmed that spring was on the way, and came home.

We were surprised by the public response. People called, wrote letters, asked questions, put up argument. Something about going to meet spring hit sensitive nerves, stirred imagination.

So the next year we went again, found spring in close to the same place, made our reports, and came home to an even greater response than we got after the first trip. I'd never received as much reader mail on anything I wrote. Most of it was favorable, although some readers thought the stories were a waste of newspaper space. (I've never been able to write a sentence that every reader liked.)

Anyway, we went again, and again. We went every spring. If we didn't leave by the second week in March, people would call and want to know if we were going, and why we were late.

Old Friend Morgan lived a part of his life in Mexico and he is the one who began calling these expeditions *Primavera*, the beautiful Spanish word for spring. To give the enterprise even greater dignity he numbered the trips with roman numerals. *Primavera* IX. *Primavera* XIV.

We went all the way through XVIII before a health problem forced O.F. to miss *Primavera* XIX. The day I am writing this, he is not running any foot races but he's up and about. He has been for me a highly satisfactory friend. He knows the words to a thousand Mexican songs and sings them on tune as we go down the road. And at unpredictable times he tells splendid stories.

People ask, "But what do you do, when you find spring?"

We celebrate it. We establish its line according to the mesquites, and with arm-waving and hosannas and other joyful noises we leave winter and go below the line into spring. Sometimes we go back and forth, returning to winter a few hours, then dropping back down into spring. We stop at nice places and sit in the warm sun, and become restored. It's close to a religious experience.

One year we did go to church, in the South Texas Brush Country town of Hebbronville. O.F. is a Catholic person and needed to attend Mass at Our Lady of Guadalupe Church and we got up at five a.m. and went, in the dark. I liked it, although I understood one word in maybe fifty because the entire service was in Spanish. A large percentage of citizens in that part of Texas are Hispanic and they like their church services in the language they speak at home. It doesn't make any difference to O.F. He hears Spanish the same as English.

When we left the church and got back on the road, I asked O.F. if he prayed during the service. He said he did. I know O.F. well enough that I can ask him such questions, which are none of my business. I wondered what he asked for when he prayed, because I am curious about matters of this kind.

"I didn't ask for anything," he said. "I gave thanks instead."

So what did he give thanks for?

He said, "I gave thanks that the doctor at Kelly Field in San Antonio was wrong that time."

During World War II an Army doctor told O.F. he had heart trouble and gave him a medical discharge when he was twenty-two. Told him if he behaved he might live twelve years.

He has behaved, sometimes better than others, long enough now to be seventy-eight years old. Reason enough, I'd say, to get up at five o'clock and go to church at Hebbronville, or anywhere else.

We always stay in South Texas about a week and sometimes by watching the mesquites we measure the advance of spring, and calculate when it will arrive in Houston, or San Antonio, or Fort Worth. We haven't done it but I suppose if we wanted to we could issue a forecast as to when spring is due in Kansas City or Chicago, or even Montreal.

One year—I loved that year—we got permission to stay at a camphouse on Moro Ranch near the town of Asherton. This was above the spring line. We liked the camp and loitered there three nights, listening to the coyotes sing out in the brush, and when we woke up on the third morning, we were in spring. It had found us, instead of the other way around. Mesquites surrounding the camp had popped out almost overnight.

Somewhere along the way, through the eighteen years, the purpose of *Primavera* changed. Its scope has broadened.

We received so much notoriety about the trip, we saw that it was more important than we thought in the beginning. One day, just before we started out on what I think was *Primavera* VII, O.F. said, "If we didn't go south to meet spring, I doubt spring would come at all. These trips are a public service." He kept saying that until I decided to agree with him.

Isn't that wonderful? Here are two old dudes who started out worrying that they might die before spring came, and now almost twenty years later they end up in control of the planet's seasons.

A considerable number of citizens have asked to go along with us to meet spring, to make it a big party concern, to head south in a motorcade of RV's and make prearranged stops where bands would play and speeches made. A couple of high octane promoters have suggested we could make money out of *Primavera*.

But O.F. and I have said no thanks to all that lollapalooza.

We don't want anybody messing with our trips, and as a result of that attitude a few folks have labeled us a couple of grumps.

It's true. Sometimes we are grumpy old bastards. One year we placed a curse on the entire city of Eagle Pass, Texas, just because we thought a motel clerk was rude to us. We were having trouble finding spring and had drifted west, because some years spring tries to slip in from that direction instead of from the south.

We had always counted Eagle Pass our favorite Tex-Mex border town and we looked for reasons to go there. We intended to stay two nights, and spend money on meals and rooms and gasoline and gifts for our loved ones. In past years we have stimulated the economy of Eagle Pass in this very way, and that rude motel clerk hurt our feelings.

We walked out and didn't sleep in that town. We swore never to stay there again or spend any money there as long as we lived and traveled. We skipped lunch to avoid spending money in Eagle Pass. We went on to Del Rio and almost ran out of gas because we refused to buy any in Eagle Pass. O.F. had a letter to mail but he would not buy a stamp at the Eagle Pass Post Office. Instead he bought it at the Del Rio Post Office fifty-five miles on up the Rio Grande.

People said to us, "Why, you old fools, it doesn't make sense to punish an entire city just because one of its citizens was rude to you. Besides, Eagle Pass will never miss you. It won't ever know it's being punished."

Maybe not, but O.F. and I will know. We had a two-man meeting about such things. Each of us delivered lectures, pointing out that millions of grumpy old men are in the world now, and they are often accompanied by grumpy old women, some of whom are even more vindictive than their men. These people have money to spend, and their numbers are growing, and they need to be treated right.

One of the people who wanted to go with us on *Primavera* once asked, "What do you and O.F. talk about when you go down the highway?" The question led me to keep up, the next spring, with topics and on the first day they included these:

Happiness, what it is, and how to achieve it.

Hate and its influence in the world.

The proliferation of lying. O.F. said he knows people who'll climb a tree to tell a lie when they could stand flat-footed and tell the truth.

Books lately read.

Mexican songs.

Enchiladas, huevos rancheros and similar haute cuisine.

Marriage. O.F. has never married. He's afraid a wife would tell him to do what he doesn't want to do. Me, I'm not comfortable being single. I've been married all my life.

Death, and dealing with the idea of it.

Sex. But not so much the last few years.

Dead friends we loved, and the list is long.

We have critics. We've heard from a few readers who say we're dealing in trivialities, that newspapers should report events of significance.

So for the last several years we've tried to become more important. We've done this by combining our annual search for spring with other serious enterprises.

Treasure hunting, for instance.

South Texas and its Gulf shoreline is salted and peppered with buried treasure, and some of it has even been found. O.F. and I decided to go after the Treasure of the Rock Pens.

We've read about the Rock Pens ever since J. Frank Dobie put the story in his book, *Coronado's Children*, back in the thirties. In the 1870s a fellow by the name of Daniel Dunham gave a death-bed statement that he had helped bury thirty-one mule loads of silver on the bank of the Nueces River near Laredo Crossing.

All that silver was brought out of Mexico by bandits and buried there at the river, but every one of them died before they could get back to dig it up. (Texas bandits of that time were always burying precious metal and then going off and dying.) Duncan said the treasure was buried below some rocks laid out like cattle or sheep pens. People have been digging and searching for the silver ever since.

O.F. and I did a lot of research on this story. We developed a new theory on the location of the silver, and figured we could find it with the right equipment. We bought a metal detector. Not a little Mickey Mouse rig, either, but a serious machine. So serious we had to pay it out by the month.

When time came for *Primavera* we loaded up, went south, found spring as usual, then turned back north and got into a motel at Freer, where we assembled the metal detector. The site we had staked out was not far north in McMullen County.

Freer is a dusty little cow, oil and rattlesnake town in the brush of Duval County. We like to stay there. People at home are always asking us, "Why do you stay in a place like Freer?" As if we ought to stay in a high-rise hotel on Ocean Drive in Corpus Christi.

We stay in certain places for particular reasons. The main reason we like Freer is that a horse is always standing out back of the Dairy Queen. I'm not sure I can make you understand why that seems important and good to us. We just like seeing that horse back there, behind a Dairy Queen.

One time we drove a hundred miles out of our way to spend a night in Alpine because a small cafe in that little city always has yellow cornbread and pinto beans cooked with salt pork.

Another time we stayed two extra nights in a motel at Del

Rio just because a waitress in the dining room had a pretty smile and was nice to us.

But getting back to the treasure. I needed to practice operating the metal detector and I did that in the motel parking lot. I discovered a metal detector draws crowds. Try it some time in a public place. People will come up and ask if you're looking for a land mine, or an oil field.

I flipped two quarters over my shoulder as a test for locating metal but before I could turn around and start detecting, two small boys out of the crowd had snatched up the coins. However, I did locate a beer bottle cap and a rusty bolt, so we took off for the Nueces River to search for the thirty-one mule loads of silver.

On the way we decided to pledge that we would give to charity a large percentage of whatever we found. We felt this promise would bring down nods and smiles from above, and improve our chances of finding the loot.

O.F. borrowed my notebook to write this pledge out, so we could both sign it and make it binding. He wrote, and we studied the language. We agreed that maybe the promise to give fifty per cent of the treasure to charity seemed excessive. And perhaps somewhat self-serving. "We don't want to be perceived as big shots," O.F. said, "giving away large sums to make headlines."

I saw his point, and suggested changing the fifty per cent to thirty-five. O.F. said he felt going on down to twenty-five would be even more appropriate. By the time we signed, the pledge said that no matter what we found, we would give to charity "a certain amount" of it.

I feel restricted as to what I can say about that treasure hunt. But it was successful. I'm not divulging how many mule loads of silver we found. I will say that if you've never been on a treasure hunt, and you get the chance, be sure to go because you'll always find treasure of one kind or another.

Now and then a reader asks if O.F. and I really believe in the mesquite theory. We do, of course. I would bet you a fifty dollar bill plus all the silver we found at the Rock Pens that a mature stand of mesquites will not be caught in leaf to suffer damage from a late spring freeze.

The first week of March in '94 we watched our theory undergo a test. We had been on the road five days and had already located spring near a little Jim Hogg County town called Agua Nueva, about forty miles north of the Rio Grande. But we were a little nervous about the weather.

O.F. was talking a lot about seeing so many cows lying down in the middle of the day. "It means a norther's coming," he kept saying. There were other signs. We'd heard coyotes howling after sunup, and that's a folk weather sign of rain.

We turned on the radio, which we almost never use on *Primavera*, and checked the reports. Amarillo was getting snow. The weather people were talking about a freeze for Houston, and the chances of damaging frost as far down the coast as Kingsville and possibly on into the Lower Rio Grande Valley. If that happened, our leafed-out mesquites would get popped and our theory would collapse in ruins. So we went to bed that night a little concerned.

But it didn't happen. That threat played out well above our line. We stayed down in spring two extra nights, to celebrate. O.F. sang several excellent songs, including *You Tell Her 'Cause I Stutter Too Much*, *Second-Hand Rose*, and one of my favorites, *I Love To Go Swimmin' With Bowlegged Women*.

Right now I'm not certain that *Primavera* has come to its close. If it has, it's been a good trip. And I can say this about the mesquites. In all those years, they've never been wrong about spring.   ∾

2.

Bowling Bottles

At the grocery store I got into a conversation with one of the customers who invited me to show up at his Kiwanis Club meeting and make a talk. He said, "You could tell the World War II story about the fellow who broke all those whiskey bottles in the barracks."

I didn't go talk at the Kiwanis because I don't make speeches any longer, and even when I was making them I didn't make any that amounted to much. But I was interested in how that gent knew about the whiskey bottles because I don't remember ever printing that story.

"I don't know whether you printed it, either," he said. "I heard you tell it one night, in a bar way out on Westheimer."

That didn't sound right to me because I don't believe I was ever in a bar on Westheimer, or at least not one that's way out, and even if I was I don't think I'd be there telling World War II stories. Because in bars, and restaurants, and similar public places it is my policy to sit and listen and not talk.

"It happened up at Sheppard Field, at Wichita Falls," said the gent in the grocery store, talking about the whiskey bottle story.

No, no, not Sheppard Field. It happened at Scott Field, Ill., early along in the war.

"And you were a buck private," the gent said.

101

I was lower than that. I was living in a one-story tar paper barracks with about forty other guys and we'd all recently washed out of pilot training in Arizona. When you washed out of pilot training you were immediately reduced far lower in rank than a buck private. You became the saddest of all sacks. The lowest form of military life.

"You felt sorry for yourselves," said the gent, prompting me, trying to make me remember what I'm unable to forget.

Worse than that. We didn't count ourselves worth being sorry for. We were all failures, rejects. Our buddies were back in Arizona, flying, getting ready to go overseas, to roar off into the wild blue yonder and become swaggering heroes, and here we were doing KP and pushing GI brooms and tromping through gray snow.

"Come on, gray snow?"

Gray snow. This was in winter and snow was everywhere, days old, some of it weeks old, and soot from stoves and furnaces settled on the snow and made it gray and ugly. I remember thinking gray snow was appropriate to the condition of our morale.

"But what about the whiskey bottles?" said my prompter.

Don't rush me. Only reason this story is worth telling, it demonstrates how low the spirits of young men can sink when they are in personal misery. When we weren't scrubbing pots and pans on KP, they had us walking the streets of the reservation, pushing GI brooms. We couldn't go to town. We were the same as imprisoned. When we were off duty we lay in our bunks and stared at the ceiling, looking for bitter pleasure in our despair.

His name was Boyd.

He was from West Virginia. An intense fellow with glaring eyes. On the night of the whiskey bottles he'd done duty at the officers' club. For one of our gang, duty at the officers club meant scrubbing floors, or the equivalent.

While cleaning up late he'd sneaked a bottle from the bar and he was quietly drunk when he came in that night carrying a barracks bag. It was full of empty whiskey bottles from the officers' club bar.

He put down the bag near the front door. He took a foot locker and carefully placed it at the far end of the aisle between the bunks. Back to his bag, then, looking neither to the right nor left. Saying nothing.

He fished an empty bottle from the bag, held it in front of his face like a bowler aiming, and sent it skidding along the floor to crash against the foot locker. Then another, and another. Angry old Boyd, bowling whiskey bottles in the night.

There was silence, other than the shattering of glass. Those of us in the bunks simply watched, with what I remember as casual interest. We understood. He didn't know what else to do or say so he just broke bottles in the barracks and maybe it made him feel a little better.

When he finished bowling the bottles he collapsed on his bunk and the others of us got brooms and cleaned up the glass. Boyd didn't help, and that was okay. I guess we felt he was breaking bottles for us all.

Not the kind of story you would tell at a Kiwanis Club. ❧

He Called Her Linda

*D*uring the holidays one of my visiting grandchildren asked me, "What's it like being old, Papa?" My answer follows:

On a recent morning I rolled out of the quilts at six o'clock and I was feeling pretty fair. The morning was crisp and clear and I was hurting in only two places, which I now consider a tolerable number. So I decided to run a few simple errands. They were these:

Drive to the bank and deposit my paycheck. Stop at the post office to mail some letters. Haul the Christmas tree to Memorial Park to be recycled. And finally, go by the supermarket for bread, milk, oatmeal and orange juice. I prepared a list of those groceries because I can never remember more than two items.

First I went out and loaded the Christmas tree on the pickup, which is handy for such jobs. Then I returned to the house to go in and get what I needed to complete my errands.

The house was locked.

This means I had locked it when I went out to load the tree, though I had no recollection of doing it, and I didn't have my keys to get in. Ah, wait, maybe I left my keys in the truck when I opened it to get my gloves before I loaded the tree.

Yes, there they were, lying on the seat. But the truck was

locked. I am always locking things out of habit and I don't even know I'm doing it.

Never mind, I've been locking keys in vehicles for fifty years and I always carry a spare key in my billfold. So I rescued the keys and came back in the house to get my grocery list, my bank stuff, and my letters to mail.

I couldn't find my glasses.

Searched for them fifteen minutes. No luck. Decided to go on without them. On bright days I can see as well without as with them, and sometimes better.

As I was driving away my neighbor was backing out and we waved and it occurred to me I couldn't remember her name. I have lived next door to that woman five years and called her name dozens of times but suddenly I couldn't remember it.

At the post office I got my business done without incident and when I was getting back in the truck I saw a fellow coming out and he looked exactly like Forrest Bassett.

I went to school with Forrest Bassett when we were boys in overalls. He had two sisters. One was Elsie and the younger one was Beth. I have not seen these people in sixty years, or thought about them in fifty, but I remember that Forrest always batted cow-handed and Elsie was good in arithmetic.

At the bank I parked and thought how interesting it is that I'm always seeing people who look like friends I haven't seen in centuries. Maybe it would be a column idea, so I found a piece of paper in the truck and made a note so I wouldn't forget it.

Guess what. I was looking in the pistol pocket for a pencil and found my glasses in there.

But a voice spoke in my ear and said I'd already written a couple of years ago about seeing strangers who look like old friends. So I wadded up the piece of paper and dropped it in the litter bag.

Went in the bank where I called out "Hello, Judy" to a loan officer. Her name is Linda. Judy is the neighbor whose name I couldn't recall when she was backing out of the driveway.

At the supermarket I couldn't find my grocery list. I believe now it was the piece of paper I discarded after I wrote the column idea on it.

I remembered the orange juice and bread but couldn't think of oatmeal or milk, because I was distracted by a nice price on canned black-eyed peas and I stocked up on those. One thing we won't need at our house for a long time is canned black-eyed peas.

But I did have to go back for milk, and whatever else it was that I'd forgotten. Called home and asked. Oh yeah. Oatmeal.

I didn't remember to deliver the Christmas tree, either, and it's still riding in the pickup.

Told my grandson that's partly what it's like, being old. But he had lost interest long before, and was watching a Denzel Washington movie on TV.   ❧

A Fish Story

*T*his is a story told to me by a young fellow with the first name of Herman. He said he didn't care if I used his full name, but I decided to do him a favor and call him only Herman. I'm not certain the story is entirely true, but I am a sucker for a story, fiction or fact, as long as it's not harmful. Also I love a mystery and we have one here. Herman was twenty-five when this story began.

Go back to the Fourth of July in 1991. Herman took a party boat out of Freeport and rode into the Gulf to fish at the snapper banks. Some of his luck was good, and some bad. The good luck was that he caught a lot of fish. The bad was that he caught a hook in his finger.

Damage to the finger wasn't great but after the hook was removed the finger began swelling so Herman removed his ring. When he tried to put the ring in his pocket, the damaged finger caused him to fumble and the ring went overboard.

Which just about ruined Herman's fishing trip, because that ring was special. It was a lodge ring that had belonged to Herman's great grandfather, whose initials JHC were engraved inside the band. The ring had been passed down through the generations. Herman's father had worn it, and so had his grandfather. Herman was the fourth wearer of the ring, and he had lost it.

Skip a year now, to the Fourth of July, 1992. Herman says he had no premonition, no mysterious voice telling him to go. He simply decided to go fishing again out of Freeport that day. He took the same boat.

He didn't catch many fish but he cranked up a couple of big snapper. Back on shore, he watched carefully when the fish cleaners butchered his catch. And you know what happened—in the belly of one of those snappers he found the ring, of course.

But wait. It wasn't the right ring. That is, it was not the ring of Herman's grandfather.

It was a 1987 high school graduation ring, from a small school in Illinois, showing the initials EMJ. Herman made phone calls and wrote letters and established from school records the ownership of the ring. Her name was Elizabeth.

Her mother was secretary to the principal of the high school where she was graduated in '87. Where was Elizabeth? She was a registered nurse, working in Chicago. Elizabeth's mother doubted the ring story. She refused to give her daughter's address or phone number to a stranger calling from Texas. Herman gave the mother his number, asked her to urge Elizabeth to call him.

When she called, Herman asked when she went fishing at the snapper banks in the Gulf. Elizabeth said she didn't know what he was talking about, that she had never seen the Gulf of Mexico. Herman told her about the ring, identified it. Elizabeth said she had dropped the ring off an excursion boat in Lake Michigan in 1988. Herman mailed it to her.

The two began corresponding, calling, speculating. How did a ring dropped in Lake Michigan end up inside a salt water fish swimming off the Texas coast? Maybe it was sucked up by a dredge? Carried out to sea? Dumped? Swallowed by a traveling fish? Could the ring have passed through several fish, and the last one was the snapper in the Gulf?

Sharing this mystery made Herman and Elizabeth friends by mail and by phone. Then in '93 he went to see her. They got along so well, they sat in restaurants and held hands and laughed about it. In October of that year they were married.

The next July, they flew out to the West Coast on vacation. They were in San Francisco. On their third day Elizabeth went shopping, left Herman sleeping.

She came in looking flushed. "Your grandfather's ring, that you dropped in the Gulf? What were his initials?"

Herman said, "JHC."

She handed Herman a ring. She had bought it for ten dollars at a little shop in Chinatown where fish were cleaned, and sold, and where the shopkeeper had on sale a variety of curious objects taken out of fish bellies. There were money clips, military dog tags, silver dollars, pocketknives, and a clutch of jewelry.

Among the jewelry was the lodge ring showing the initials JHC inside the band. ∞

Turkey for One

Did I ever tell you about the time I cooked a Thanksgiving dinner, all by myself?

I believe it was in '81, not long after I'd been cut loose in the world to do my own cooking and laundry and housekeeping. A condition that lasted several long years.

That was a strange time for me because I had never been alone, ever. Some things about living alone I liked pretty well, but I did get lonesome now and then and especially on holidays when all my friends were mixed up in family doings.

If you are alone in the world you may have a multitude of friends, but there'll still be times when not one of them is available to help dispel the loneliness. And even though kind people will ask you to take part in their family festivities you know you'll feel like an intruder, so you refuse such invitations because you'd rather be alone than to be where you're not comfortable.

So that Thanksgiving morning of '81 I was walking the floors of a two-room apartment, and feeling as if I was the only person alive on the premises. An apartment house, where so many single people live, can get mighty empty on family-type holidays because the singles so often go home, or at least somewhere else.

I remember talking to myself, aloud, about how I might get

through the day. One, I could go over to the cafeteria and eat Thanksgiving dinner with the AARP crowd that gathered there. Nice people, but they talked mostly about arthritis and grandchildren and Social Security, and that was beginning to depress me.

Or I could go eat alone at a restaurant, and I was already tired of doing that.

Another option was to get mildly drunk, which sometimes helped pass a lonesome day, but there were side effects to consider. I'd watched a procession of washed-out husbands disappear into the jug and I didn't want to follow that sad parade.

Then I remembered a magazine piece I'd read while sitting in my dentist's outer office. The writer had just endured a divorce and she described a test she'd made, about living alone. The test was that she cooked a five-course meal for herself, and ate it alone, and enjoyed it, which told her she was surviving, that she'd be okay.

That seemed worth a try.

I drove outside the Loop and bought a turkey, smallest one I could find. Frozen hard as steel. I got some other things that seemed like Thanksgiving. Potatoes. Celery. Onions. Green beans. Cranberry sauce. I can't remember what else.

Brought all that stuff back to the apartment and spread it out. I called a lady I was married to once, a good cook, to ask her what to do next. She didn't answer.

Okay. First problem was a utensil for cooking the turkey. Biggest I had then was a large bean pot I got out of Osa Lee Jones' Seagull Restaurant at San Leon, after the restaurant closed. About a four-gallon vessel.

It wouldn't go in the oven so I drew water into it and set it on top of the stove and dumped the turkey in there and turned on the burner. Cookbooks say you ought to thaw out frozen poultry before you cook it, but I proved on that Thanksgiving Day that it's not necessary.

But it does take longer.

Around noon I cut a drumstick off and it wasn't anywhere near done. I threw it back and poured in a couple of beers. I peeled the potatoes and quartered them and added lots and lots of seasoning, such as pepper and salt and some other stuff somebody had given me when they heard I was going to keep house alone. It was dark green, I remember that.

Later on, during half-time of the football game, I remembered the onions and the celery and the green beans, so I chopped them up and pitched them in with the turkey and everything else.

At the end of the third quarter I took the turkey out of the pot and cut into it and it was still half raw. But it was easier to cut, and I carved it into about eight parts and put them all back in the pot and I poured in another beer or two. I noticed a curious wax paper package that came out of the middle of that bird. This turned out to be the giblets, which I gave to a tomcat that came around begging free meals.

Time the game was over I had myself a kind of turkey stew. It was not wonderful but it was not bad, and lasted five days. I had the can of cranberry sauce for dessert. ❧

Skinning Arnold

$\mathcal{T}$he other night we went to see the Arnold Schwarzenegger movie, "Terminator 2: Judgment Day." By the end of it I was disappointed because the steel-making plant didn't explode and light up the heavens for two hundred miles around and wipe the city off the face of the planet. I wanted more violence.

I was surprised at myself because I wasn't much interested in violence when we went in the theater. But the shooting and the crashing started early and pretty soon I got used to it, and after the first hour I didn't mind it.

Then I began to look for when the next wave of it was coming, and to predict what it would be. I mean like maybe it would be a lot more glass shattering when Arnold picked up a person, with one hand, and heaved the person through another window. Or it might be an additional two or three police cars getting blown up. Or Arnold getting shot in the face. He got shot in the face quite a few times.

Along about the middle of the show Arnold skinned his arm and hand, and I was able to watch that without grinding my teeth. So then I saw I was getting into the spirit. After the skinning of the arm, nothing bothered me.

Wait, I don't mean he skinned his arm the way a kid might skin a knee falling off a bicycle. I say to you he skinned his arm the way a hunter skins a dead deer. By peeling all the hide off it, from just below the elbow all the way to the tips of his fingers.

He did this to show the stuff he was made of, which was metal, and hinges, and circuits, and things like that. He is what they call a cyborg. You scratch a cyborg and you get hardware.

So it didn't hurt him to peel his arm and hand that way, and there wasn't a whole lot of blood because Arnold's kind of cyborg doesn't have your standard supply. Near as I could tell, he bled only skin deep.

People who frequently go to movies will see from this report that I am not well acquainted with Arnold Schwarzenegger pictures. I had to look up what a cyborg is. Dictionary says it's a human who has certain bodily processes controlled by cybernetically operated devices. Meaning controlled by computer.

In this show, Arnold is a good cyborg. There is also a bad one and he is more advanced than Arnold in the matter of doing bad stuff, due to the computer chip that operates him. It's a mighty wonderful chip, I tell you that.

From six feet you could shoot a hole in that dude the size of a dishpan, and it would seem to disarrange him, but in a minute he has put himself back together again. And mean as a snake, same as before.

There was this woman in the picture and the most extraordinary thing she did was have a dream in which her city was destroyed, I guess by a nuclear blast. Everything in the path of the fire storm was cremated, including her own little baby. Isn't that nice?

When the blast came she was holding onto a chain-link fence. The fire storm took all her flesh off and left her skeleton standing there with its finger bones laced into the wires of the fence.

By that time I was so into violence that my thought was, Hey, that woman's sure got sturdy bones, because her skeleton is still standing against a blast that has vaporized tall buildings. A pretty strong fence, too, now I think of it.

But that was just a dream.

Getting back to reality, toward the end of the story the bad cyborg was knocked into a great vat of molten metal in a steel-making plant, and this melted him. But he didn't melt easy.

He kept rising out of the bubbling metal, writhing, screaming, showing us the various forms he had assumed since early in the picture. Once he came up with an open mouth, which turned inside out, and there were other forms of him down in his throat.

I supposed that for a finale, the entire world would explode and finish all of us off. I discovered that I was looking for it, maybe even hoping it would happen. But it didn't. Only thing that happened was, Arnold committed suicide by sinking into the hot metal, and he didn't quiver or utter a syllable. It seemed like a cop-out to me, after two hours of shuddering destruction.

The message I got out of the film was, we can be exposed to so much violence that eventually we become calloused, and violence doesn't mean much unless it's worse than what we've already seen.

This is the most expensive and one of the more popular movies ever made. I think everybody ought to see it.   ∾

Max the Optimist

*Y*ou see this dog, snoring here by my foot? That's my friend Max. You might want to meet him. He's a little squirrely but he's all right. He's interesting, and he's educational. I've learned things of value from this dog.

Tell you what I'll do. Make you a deal. You sit still while I tell you about my dog, and next time I see you I'll be quiet and you can tell me about yours. It's a swap. Equal time, okay?

This animal is a yellow Lab. Three years old. He's no Rhodes scholar but he compensates for his lack of intelligence with an overdose of the characteristic that governs his life:

He's a pluperfect optimist.

You're looking at eighty-five pounds of four-footed, brown-eyed, tail-wagging optimism. When he gets up in the morning Max thinks something wonderful is about to happen to him before breakfast. And if not, by at least ten o'clock, and if not then, at least by noon.

This dog is a purebred Lab and his papers show he was named *Canis Maximus*. I think he ought to be registered as *Canis Optimus*.

You want a clue? Watch this.

I now raise my arms and put the palms of my hands on the arms of this chair and push up, just a little way, as if I'm about to rise. Immediately Max pops to attention. Legs locked. Head and ears high. Tail wiggling.

He expects that I'm going to stop working and do something he thinks will be fun. Such as going for a walk. Or we might be about to take a break and throw and fetch tennis balls. Out in the yard, where he can leave his signature on all the trees and shrubs, every one of which he has signed dozens of times before.

But all I'm about to do is walk six steps to the coffee pot.

Do you think Max is disappointed? He is not. Disappointment is a negative proposition and it's not in his data base. He doesn't sulk. He doesn't complain. He waddles around here with a grin on his muzzle, huffing and grunting about how great it is to be alive and to have creatures who love him. I can see him saying, "It's all right. Drink your coffee. Maybe in a few minutes we'll go out."

If you keep up with these reports, you'll recall that sometimes I mention the old country house in Washington County where we often hide out. Max is happiest there. He is so glad to go, it's almost more than he can bear. He'll stand out in the yard, trembling with passion, trying to tell us, "Isn't this fine, just being here?" Then he'll break and run in tight circles, at amazing speeds, demonstrating how happy he is to be in that primitive place.

When his mother and father produced him, they intended Max to be a retriever. They thought he'd be swimming through icy waters to bring back fallen ducks to hunters. Too bad that he was sold into a family that doesn't shoot things.

But he's a splendid retriever, anyhow. He just doesn't retrieve dead birds. Instead he retrieves sticks, and tennis balls, and Frisbees and anything else you want to fling, and he'll keep retrieving as long as your throwing arm lasts.

He has highly sensitive ears. What he listens for is the crinkle of wrapping paper. He thinks that sound always means somebody is unwrapping a loaf of bread, which is his favorite thing to eat.

I've tested him by placing chunks of bread on a plate, and chunks of meat on another plate nearby. He eats the bread every time, and looks around for more, and if he can't find additional bread he'll condescend to eat meat. Without fear of contradiction, I could quote this animal as saying it may be true that man cannot live by bread alone, but a dog can.

Christmas morning is a frustration for Max, with all that crinkling of paper going on when gifts are unwrapped. He's puzzled when a person unwraps a shirt, or a book, or a bottle of perfume, because he expects everything wrapped up ought to be bread.

Max is interested in romance but the nearest he has to a mate is a black female Lab, a middle-aged spinster who also lives with us. Due to surgery when she was just a girl, she will be forever barren. But Max refuses to accept even this hopeless circumstance. Every morning for two years he has proposed to this black-haired lady, who has told him hundreds of times she's simply not interested.

But Max won't quit hoping. His philosophy is that in this life you've got to look for goodness and wonders. You've got to believe.　　　　　　　　　　　　　　　　　　ew

How to Quit

"**Y**ou'll have to give me credit for one thing," he said. "I knew when to quit, and how to do it."

That was my friend Mel talking. He came by to drink my coffee and read my paper. He was commenting on his recent retirement from a job he'd held for thirty years.

What generated the remark about knowing when to quit was the story out of Dallas, prominent lately in the news. It's about the preacher who resigned because the preacher whose place he took wouldn't go away and let the new one run the show.

"It reminds me of when I came out of school and took my first job," Mel said, and got up to refill his cup. "The day I reported for work, they introduced me to an old guy called Mr. Fuller. They gave me a desk next to his and told me he was retiring in two weeks and I would take his place.

"They said he had a lot of holdover vacation coming and he could walk out at any time, but he'd agreed to stick around for a couple of weeks and show me the ropes.

"I could tell Mr. Fuller didn't like me. He asked a bunch of questions like where I came from, and what jobs I'd had, and he wasn't too happy with my answers.

"He said a college education was all right, in certain cases, but he believed the best education came out of the school of hard knocks. He was always talking about the school of hard knocks. Don't you ever buy any coffee cream?"

Told him no, I read the other day that cow's milk might not be good even for babies, so how could it be good for adults?

He said, "You need something to cut this stuff, if you're gonna keep using stale coffee. Anyhow, about Mr. Fuller. He was one of these old boys who came out of retirement during World War II, when all the young guys were shipped off to be cannon fodder. When I went to work there he was seventy-eight if he was a day. I felt like I was working with my grand-father. Not that I did much work with him.

"The first two weeks, he didn't really show me a blamed thing about how to do the work. He did it all himself, and once in a while he would show it to me after it was done, and tell me how they did it when he was coming up in the school of hard knocks.

"I was relieved when they came around to collect five dollars from me, to help buy Mr. Fuller a present to give him at his retirement party. I was glad to donate. I would have given ten dollars if I'd had it.

"They threw a big party for him right there in the office. Cake and punch and decorations and everybody making speeches about how Mr. Fuller kept the home fires going all during the war, when it was way past time for him to sit back and rest.

"President of the company showed up for the party, and all the girls in the office put kisses on Mr. Fuller's jaw, and he made a speech about the school of hard knocks and everybody clapped and smiled.

"The company president gave a little talk and said what the firm needed, to whip the competition, was about two dozen more hands like Mr. Fuller. Guess what the present was, that we gave him."

I guessed a rod and reel.

"No," Mel said, "it was a rocking chair. Pretty nice one, too. When the party was over I offered to carry it down and put it in Mr. Fuller's car and he said never mind, he'd send somebody after it later on. That was on a Friday.

"Monday morning when I got to work, there was Mr. Fuller at his desk, just like always. The rocking chair was gone.

"This went on for another couple of weeks, Mr. Fuller doing what he'd always done, work I was hired to do. Finally I went to the boss and said I thought Mr. Fuller had retired. Boss said yes, but he'd asked to stay on for a while so he could gear down. He said Mr. Fuller was working without pay. Said it was hard to tell an old guy like that to get on out when he'd done such a fine job during tough times when all the good help was overseas."

So how long, I asked, did Mr. Fuller last?

Mel shrugged. "I don't know. I quit after six months, and he was still there. I learned something from that."

Like what?

"When I got ready to retire," Mel said, "I remembered Mr. Fuller, and I spent a week with the young guy who replaced me. He was so stupid. He knew nothing. I gave him my number and told him to call if he needed me.

"That was more than a year ago," Mel said, "and he's never called once."   ∽

A Two Dollar Goat

*Y*ou've caught me on the front porch of the old country house in Washington County, where I am considering a proposition made to me at the post office in Round Top.

A fellow wearing dark glasses and a feed store cap offered to sell me a couple of Spanish goats for two dollars apiece. I told him no thanks, but while I was driving back out here to our little patch of woods that goat proposition kept getting more and more interesting.

No, I don't mean that I'm about to change my mind and buy those goats. What stays with me is the question of why the man would sell them for such an attractive price. It's been a long time since I kept a watch on the livestock market but I'm fairly sure that two dollars for a goat is low.

I think now of a proverb quoted often by my Uncle Billy Crockett, long ago up in Palo Pinto County. "Ain't no such animal as a five dollar mule."

What that meant to Uncle Billy was that if a man offers to sell you a mule for five dollars you had better examine that animal mighty close before you part with your money because the mule is apt to be blind in one eye, and maybe both, or have a lame leg, or various bad habits, such as pitching in harness, or knowing how to open gates. So that in the final accounting a mule bought for five dollars will end up costing far more than he is worth.

Remembering Uncle Billy's cautionary proverb has me thinking now that there may not be any such animal as a two dollar goat.

At post offices in little Texas towns like Round Top a patron speaks often to many citizens he is not acquainted with, and I have not yet been introduced to the gent who made me the offer. But I could find him with little trouble if I needed to, because we have very few people around here dealing in Spanish goats. In fact, I will be surprised if the man fails to find me, to follow up on his sales pitch, and so I need to be ready for him or else I might end up owning a couple of animals that I don't want.

He already has an advantage over me. Which is, I don't know anything at all about him, and he knows a good deal about me and my situation here on this little reservation.

He knows, for example, that pretty soon I'll have to do something about the brush on this place because it is moving in on us, creeping closer and closer to the house, and eventually I'll have to use a cane knife to hack my way through the jungle to reach the front gate.

So here's this stranger, all friendly and courteous, coming up to me at the post office and saying he sees I have a brush problem and it just happens he has goats that will take care of it very efficiently, at a price of only two dollars per head.

When you are a city dweller who has come out like this and bought a little rural real estate, you must expect that the local folks will know in a short time a great deal about you and your property, even though you have not met them or spoken to them or even waved at them.

They will know where your place is, and who you bought it

from, and how much you paid, and probably whether you were able to write a check for the entire acreage or had to borrow the money.

They will know things about the old house that's on the land you bought. They'll know who was born in it, and who died in it and from what cause. They'll know who built the house and whether he was a good carpenter or not.

They'll know things about your land that you may never find out, unless you ask them. They'll know what used to be grown on it, and who grew it, and what the soil is suited for. They might tell you there's no use planting grapes, or roses, or whatever, but they won't tell you unless you ask.

So they know all these things, and therefore you mustn't be surprised if a stranger comes up at the post office and says he's noticed you have a brush problem and offers to sell you goats.

The fact is I've thought of bringing in a few browsers to work on our brush but the trouble is, the fence around this place is barbed wire, and getting over a five-strand barbed wire fence is about as much trouble for a Spanish goat as it is for a jay bird. So I would need a goat-proof fence.

The only thing I've been able to figure is, it may be that the gent selling those two dollar goats is in the fence-building business. ∾

In the Pew of the Prominents

Back in my old hometown we had a clan we called the Easter Family, which wasn't their real name. We called them that because they came to church only on Easter Sunday.

They weren't the only members of that church who showed up once a year, but they were the most spectacular. They were handsome people and they always had new clothes at Easter and looked really elegant.

They had strength of numbers, too. When they arrived in force, must have been fifteen or twenty of them. Filled an entire pew, which sometimes caused problems as I will tell you farther down.

The Easter Family was simply different from the regulars. They always wanted to sit together. Even their teen-agers sat with the parents, which in our church was considered abnormal.

A lot of the regular members had unkind remarks to make in private about the Easter Family. A common criticism was that the family didn't really care anything about church, that all they wanted to do was march down the aisle on Easter to show off their new clothes.

One reason I have not forgotten the Easter Family after all

this time is that my father was a fan of theirs. On Easter Sunday morning he would be stirring around early, telling us all to hurry up, hurry up, because he didn't want to miss the entrance of the Easter Family. He was interested in clothes. For many years he sold clothes for a living, and he admired sharp dressers. He was a sharp dresser himself.

Our mother would tell him that going to church to see people in finery was not in the spirit of Easter, that we really ought to wear our plainest clothes, like Jesus wore homespun robes.

My father would come back with, "Well, then how come you went out and spent two dollars for a new hat? Why don't you wear the hat you bought five years ago?"

"That's not the point," she would say.

But it seemed to me it was the point.

Anyway, what I started out to tell you is about the time the Easter Family sat in the pew of the Prominents. Nobody ever spoke publicly about this but certain pews in our church were reserved for certain families. No signs were put on them but the regulars knew not to sit in these pews because certain people had been sitting in them ever since our town quit having gunfights and started having church instead.

It was common to say that you could earn a reserved pew by giving money to the church and I think that was the truth but not all of it. You could also earn a reserved seat by showing up for every service. Sunday morning. Sunday night. And Wednesday prayer meeting. Year after year. World without end, amen.

The Prominent Family had earned a pew both ways, by giving money and by being faithful attenders, a mighty strong claim. I am calling them the Prominent Family here because that was just about the most exalting adjective any family could hope to hear, modifying its name.

On this Easter Sunday I am remembering, we were there early enough for my father to enjoy watching the Easter Family parade in. Its women were something, smiling and gliding down the aisle in pink and white and lavender and pale blue, and giving off sweet smells.

You could almost hear gasps when they chose a pew, side-stepped in, stood a moment to be admired, and seated themselves in unison—in the pew of the Prominents. My father jabbed me on the knee with his thumb. "Watch this," the jab said.

The Prominents always came in late. A show of confidence, I think, that their place would be waiting. But on this Sunday it was not.

Later, at Easter dinner, we talked about that extraordinary scene, which had upset our mother. My father thought it was wonderful.

He said we had witnessed uncommon events: The Prominents, filing down the aisle to claim their pew, and finding it not only full but full of people who came to church only once a year. And the Easter Family sitting there with self-pleased smiles, not knowing they had committed the first cousin to a high-grade felony. And the Prominents, mortified, forced to march back up the aisle and sit in the balcony which was about the same as the right-field bleachers in a ball park.

Of course all this was long ago, and people aren't like that any more. Are they?   ∾

Chester Went Poof

*T*he other evening I attended storytelling time at my neighborhood ice house where the main event was Red Woman's account of how her third husband Chester disappeared when he went out in the yard to pick up the paper.

The one they call Red Woman, due to the spectacular color of her hair, is an amiable person of middle age who is a regular at the ice house and who is known for her charitable works, such as loaning five bucks to needy parties, and taking bread and milk and beer to nice old ladies who are unable to get out and around for necessities.

It is told by the other ice house regulars that Red Woman can talk half a day without telling a lie, and I accept this proposition. I have heard her talk for half a day, so I know she can do that much, at least, and I have no reason that would stand up in court to doubt she is giving out anything but gospel about the strange disappearance of her husband Chester.

I have listened to the story maybe four times and it does seem a few details differ from one telling to the next, but that must be expected of a worthwhile story. What I say is that if a storyteller like Red Woman has a winner that has kept an audience at attention for fourteen years, she will be an insult to the trade if she can't improve the thing from one performance to the next.

Chester's disappearance dates back to September of 1980, and a couple of regulars at the ice house knew him well. I did not, as I was operating in another region at that time and listening to other stories, but the regulars have filled me in on Chester's history.

He called himself a cabinetmaker, and he did have tools appropriate to that craft but the regulars say Chester was bad about working, meaning he often stayed home when other members of his trade were out making cabinets. He also was frequently injured on the job, although the injuries were vague, and the jobs, as well.

Anyhow, back in '78 Chester and Red Woman showed up married, to the great surprise of all the regulars, but a party was thrown in their honor at the ice house for it was customary for parties to be thrown there for all of Red Woman's marriages.

Chester's disappearance came about at nine p.m. on the thirteenth of September in 1980. He was in his easy chair watching a wrestling match when Red Woman asked him to go outside and fetch the evening paper, as she was suffering from a cold and had not gone out for the paper according to her custom. This was when we had an afternoon paper in this town.

So Chester went forth, despite that he had recently complained about a serious leg injury. He never came back.

Here's Red Woman talking: "He didn't even have shoes on. He was in his work socks. He had on his khaki pants but just an undershirt, which is how he watched TV, with his feet on the coffee table. He left half a beer on the table when he went out. He also left a cigarette burning in the ash tray. I'd given him his supper which was my nice meatloaf with hot rolls and butter.

"The last thing he said to me, he said, 'All right, all right, I'll get the paper,' and he went out and left the front door open, and I never saw him again. It's like he went poof, and disappeared.

"After five minutes I went out to see about him. There was nothing. No sign of violence. No footprints. Nothing. The evening paper was not there. I went to all the neighbors, asking. Nobody saw him.

"I went to the police, missing persons, all the things you can do. Chester has a son in Florida but he has not seen his daddy in twenty years and he was no help, wouldn't talk to me."

Red Woman's story always ends with the line, "Something strange happened to Chester. Something got him."

New customers at the ice house who hear this story shrug and say, well, probably Chester was simply ready to cut out, and he ran off. But those who knew Chester say, no way. They say he might run off without his shoes, or without his shirt, but it's impossible that Chester would walk off and leave half a cold beer sitting on the coffee table.

Red Woman was something like forty when Chester disappeared. She comes to the ice house now with a smiling gent by the name of Oscar and they have been together, as the saying is, for ten years. Red Woman will tell you they have not married because she still expects that one of these times Chester will show up at the front door, in his sock feet and undershirt, and maybe with the paper in his hand. ∽

What He Stole

$\mathcal{E}$arly Monday morning, before six-thirty, I saw the most interesting sight I've seen in recent times. If you will sit still a couple of minutes I would like to tell you about it.

The beginning of it was a phone call from my kids. They are trying to sell the house that they grew up in, and they were cleaning it out. They had stacked up about two hundred volumes of old books that belonged to me. If I wanted them, they would load them up and bring them to me.

I wanted at least to go through the books and so they brought them to the country place in Washington County. We sat on the front porch and had a good time, rummaging through a lot of my old stuff that they brought in addition to the books. They'd also brought half a dozen old suitcases that nobody wanted. So we used them for boxes. Filled them with the books I culled out of the load.

This is why I got back into Houston Sunday night with six suitcases full of books in the back of my station wagon. I intended, and still do, to find somebody who wants them. I never throw old books away, since I was taught early that you can go to hell for that. But I was tired and didn't unload Sunday night. A suitcase full of books is mighty heavy.

Next morning early I felt stronger so I brought the wagon around and parked it on the street near my back door. That way I wouldn't have to lug those suitcases very far. I took one suitcase in and found a place for it, and then my coffee-water pot was whistling so I stopped to fix a cup. I was a little longer getting back out to the car than I planned.

When I got back outside I saw a stocky little man hurrying around the corner carrying a great suitcase. He carried it in both arms, the way a guy holds a load that's near his weight limit. Took me a few seconds to realize that I had left the tailgate open and he had taken one of my suitcases out of the station wagon. This was the extraordinary sight I mentioned in the first paragraph—that person going around the corner with my suitcase.

What did I do? Nothing. I stood there and thought about it a while, before I started grinning. This thief had stolen a suitcase I didn't want, and it was full of books I intended to give away.

I went back in and sat on the sofa and tried to see how it happened. The guy has to be a minor league thief or else he won't be on foot. He's walking the streets early in the morning, maybe even working garbage dumpsters for grub.

He's going along my street and here's this dirty black station wagon sitting there with the tailgate open and five suitcases are stacked near the back. They yearn to be taken.

He looks all around, listens. Nobody. Nothing. Memorial Day morning. Mighty quiet. So he grabs the biggest of the suitcases and utters a hissing cuss word because that dude is so heavy.

Then he thinks, Hey, this is something special. A suitcase this heavy is bound to contain great valuables. He goes (to wherever he took it) and opens it and finds those old books and he is mighty puzzled. Books?

He decides that this makes no sense. Why would anybody

be carrying a suitcase loaded with books? There's got to be a reason. Must be something particular about these books.

So he goes through every volume, page by page. Looking for what? Drugs, maybe. He's seen movies where pages of books are knifed out and packets of narcotics put in the holes, for smuggling. Or money. Don't you remember the whodunits where books are used to hide thousand-dollar bills because the hider knew nobody would ever open a book?

I don't know what books were in the suitcase. I remember we found five paperback copies of *Huckleberry Finn* and at least three of *Moby Dick* and a couple of paperback collections of O. Henry stories and three or four paperbacks of Shakespeare. So maybe some of those were among them.

It pleases me to imagine that the thief searched in those old books so long that at last he, or maybe the children in his house, discovered the real value hidden there. ∿

A Sad Sack

*H*ere is a note from a World War II pal, Buddy Halstead, who says that the Colonel was buried last month in Chicago. Died of lung cancer at seventy-eight.

The last time I saw the Colonel was at Scott Field, Ill. I was packed and ready to board a bus and go into St. Louis and catch a train to Yuma, Ariz.

This was 1943. I was standing in front of the post exchange and the Colonel came up and borrowed a dollar to buy cigarettes. Cigarettes in the PX were selling then for something like twenty cents a pack so my dollar probably bought the Colonel a couple of days' supply. He was a big smoker.

The Colonel said his bunch would be going to Yuma before long and he'd pay me the buck when he got to Arizona.

Sure, Colonel.

We called him the Colonel as a sort of satirical nickname, the way fat guys are often called Tiny. He was a buck private, and totally unfit to be a soldier.

He always looked sick to me. Sounded sick, too, with that smoker's cough. He was thin and bony, with a permanent shoulder slump and a flat-footed way of walking. He had huge brown eyes that bulged, showing lots and lots of white.

His uniform didn't fit. Not even his underwear fit. One of those old olive drab GI undershirts hung from his bony shoulders like a rag on a fence. He seemed always to need a shave, even just after he shaved.

All the years since Scott Field, I have thought of the Colonel as the original sad sack, the permanent GI goof-off.

He hated the Army. But he was shrewd, and focused—focused on trying to avoid doing whatever his superiors wanted him to do. And he was often successful, mainly because he had help from those of us around him.

I'm not sure why we supported him. Partly because he was older, I guess. He was about twenty-nine in '43. Most guys in the barracks with him were anywhere from eighteen to twenty-two.

We were eager. We wanted in the war, so we could go home heroes, and we did pretty much as we were told. Yet we were fascinated by the Colonel's willingness to take the risks of defying authority.

After chow at night he would lecture on the Army's stupid rules, which resulted in what he called the expenditure of time and effort to no useful purpose. Morning roll call, for example.

Before dawn every day, in rain or sleet or snow or whatever, we were rolled out, to dress and go outside and stand in formation to answer a call of the roll. Sometimes you could talk a friend into answering for you, if you just couldn't coax yourself out of the sack. The Colonel almost never made roll call.

I see him in the gloomy barracks light at five a.m., rising up on an elbow, those big old eyes showing white, dog tags swinging from his skinny neck, and saying to the nearest guy, "Sing out for me, will ya, Mac?" Then falling back and pulling the GI blanket over his head.

The Colonel's principal pleasure was embarrassing self-important brass.

He was simply unable to accept that it was reasonable to

salute a commissioned officer. It pained him to do it, so he worked up this sneaky trick. It was his revenge, for the times he was unable to avoid saluting.

On the streets of St. Louis he would watch for young, fresh second lieutenants. They were easy to spot because they were forever looking for enlisted men who were supposed to salute them.

The Colonel liked to zero in on an approaching shavetail accompanied by a pretty girl. When he drew within range, the Colonel would throw up his right hand in what looked like the beginning of a salute, and quickly the lieutenant would snap off a return.

Too late, the lieutenant would see that the Colonel was not really saluting, but only bringing a cigarette up to his mouth to take a puff.

If the officer stopped to chew the Colonel out, he would say, "Why, Lieutenant, I just didn't see you." Which was a deeper insult than the lack of the salute, since all new second lieutenants wished to be highly visible.

My friend Halstead says the Colonel spent most of his life in Chicago, and at his death was identified as a retired accountant.

Some day if they really have that big roll call Up Yonder, I don't know whether the Colonel will be present to answer. But even if he's not, I'll bet the dollar he owes me that he'll have somebody there to sing out for him.   ∾

No Fuzz

$\mathcal{B}$ack on the front porch of the old country house in Washington County, and feeling a little foolish because I have let a couple of small birds make me move from my accustomed work place.

The problem is that these birds are cardinals, one of our most valued Texas songbirds, and they are near the top of the list of creatures we try to co-exist with, here in this little patch of woods. Therefore we are obliged to be inconvenienced by them.

What they did was build a nest on a live oak limb that hangs almost over the front steps. They built it while we were in Houston, trying to make enough money to pay the expenses on this place, which is the ultimate example of a non-profit enterprise. The cardinals had no idea that humans would ever be clodding around here, scaring the very feathers off them. They couldn't have dreamed, either, that we would bring with us two ninety pound cats, which happen to be dogs instead, but cardinals don't know the difference and are always willing to think the worst about anything bigger than they are.

We can't even walk out of the house without scaring the mama cardinal off her eggs. So if we pursue our normal activities, the eggs in that nest will not be sat on, no baby cardinals will hatch out of them, and this will be a violation of our law of co-existence.

That's why we are using the back door instead of the front, and trying to keep the ninety pound cats from making their fearsome noises when they trot beneath the nest. It's also why I have moved my work table to the other end of the front porch, so the gentle tapping on this computer keyboard won't sound like a machine gun to that bird, and send her off the nest in a desperate flutter.

When we passed the co-existence law we didn't actually write out a list of what we would live with and what we wouldn't. Making such a list could not be a comfortable process because it is discriminatory without shame.

Listen to this: We live with dirt daubers, but not red wasps. Bees, but not yellow jackets. Caterpillars, but not grub worms. June bugs, but not blister beetles.

We are against rats and mice but in favor of their rodent cousins, the squirrels. We don't like skunks, but raccoons we do.

We would gladly provide dens for coyotes because we love their nocturnal serenades, but most of our neighbors consider coyote a cuss word.

We want frogs, but not snakes. Crickets, but not grass-hoppers.

We accept fire ants only because we have no choice.

We live in harmony with certain spiders, such as those big yellow banana jobs with long skinny legs and speckled bodies, and a couple of other friendly species. But no spiders with fuzzy legs or bodies had better show themselves around here. We don't let fuzz in the house if it's on spiders. A few years ago I had a couple of truly poisonous letters after I reported killing a tarantula the size of a fried egg that was trying to come in the front door. Letters said tarantulas are harmless. Yes, but I simply can't love a spider with that many long legs and every one fuzzy from foot to armpit.

On birds, we want to live with cardinals, mockingbirds, doves, cuckoos, larks, blue birds, and most other kinds. We even welcome the woodpeckers that try to make holes in the side of the house, and hawks we like, and owls. But not house sparrows, cowbirds, starlings, or buzzards.

Buzzards weren't on the bad list in the beginning but then a pair of turkey vultures nested in one of our brush piles and raised a couple of babies and we happened to meet one, face to beak, and it was so ugly that ever since we have been opposed to vultures. At least those that want to live with us.

That baby buzzard didn't do anything except stand there, but it was so ugly that where it was standing the grass turned brown.

It does seem a shame to be so picky about associating with the creatures around us. But it strikes me now that the creatures themselves are even more particular. We are providing living quarters for a multitude of flying, crawling animals, and the only ones that want anything at all to do with us are the fire ants.   ∾

Friday Night Football

*L*ately I have been attending high school football games, which I had not planned to do ever again in my life.

This has come to pass because within the past year I acquired a relative who plays linebacker. And in our state if you are kin by blood or marriage to a linebacker, or an offensive tackle, or a member of the pep squad, the law is that you go to the games and you root for the team. You may need to drive halfway across Texas to do your rooting, but you have to go and root.

I had not attended any high school football games since about 1967, and when I got through attending them I celebrated and said, "Thank the angels that's over with, at last."

Now here I am doing it again.

If you've ever been connected in any official capacity to a high school football player, you already know that the connection changes your life, and there is nothing whatever you can do about it.

It changes the days you can leave town, and when you can't. It changes where you go when you do leave town. It changes what you eat at home, and when you eat it, because football players must eat certain stuff and they must eat it at certain times.

I had forgotten all the effects of having high school athletes in the house. This is the first linebacker I've had anything to do with, and my observation is that linebackers eat and drink more, and faster, than other species. How about half a gallon of orange juice a day. That may not impress anybody, but it does me.

In previous lives I fed and housed first basemen, point guards, split ends, outfielders, left-handed pitchers, and one punt-and-kickoff returner. None of those ever downed half a gallon of orange juice a day, but they had other extraordinary influences on my life, and even more expensive.

They caused me to do foolish things. Such as driving six hundred miles, non-stop, half of it in excess of the posted speed limit, so I wouldn't be late for a game one of my kids was playing in. That's pretty stupid.

But as near as I can figure, it's impossible to avoid getting swept up in high school athletics if you've got kids involved.

They don't even have to be on the team. I remember when my daughter had to attend an athletic contest one hundred miles from home, and it was a life-and-death proposition. You know why? Because she was a special friend of a dude scheduled to be the starting pitcher. She might as well have been on the roster and playing third base, so I had to take her.

In that sort of situation, parents will go almost anywhere, and sometimes not because they are all that interested in the contest but because they want their kids to get home safely.

Still, at this stage of my time, I never imagined I would get excited again about a high school football game. I confess I sort of like it.

The last couple of weeks I have discovered myself among the guys who stand up and shake their fists and shout that the game officials need to have their eyes checked if they didn't see that holding violation on the thirty-yard line.

Also I have again become critical of decisions made by coaches. I have regained my expert knowledge of the sport that I had back in the sixties when my first set of kids was playing. I can call plays better than any offensive coordinator.

Suddenly, I know football truths just as I knew them long ago. Truths like: If you've got a runner making four, six, or eight yards a pop over the middle, you better not stop inside the twenty and get cute and throw a pass into tight coverage, because you're going to get intercepted and kill the drive.

Also I have gone back to clapping my hands when the cheerleaders perform those acrobatics they ought not to perform because they're too dangerous. And when the band plays the national anthem before the kickoff I put my hand over my heart and feel the excitement beating inside me. Years ago I figured I had lost that sort of feeling forever about schoolboy sports.

Then this week I got a phone call from Alabama and heard that my ten-year-old grandson is a seventy-five pound defensive lineman for his elementary school in Mobile. So there may be no end to this, which I thought was all over twenty-five years ago.   ∾

A Mysterious Christmas Song

Once in a while they just walk up and tell you stories. This is most likely to happen at Christmas which is an emotional time and feelings rise close to the surface and they have to be expressed because they're painful to hold in.

I was in the foyer of the bank, mailing a couple of letters in the drop boxes they keep by the elevators and this woman appeared and asked if she could tell me a story. That is my favorite of all the questions I hear, so I told her go ahead, let's have the story.

She said it wasn't anything that would make a piece for the paper. She said mainly it was a feeling that had come over her, and it had to do with memories and with something that happened to her lately, something that she counted to be a personal miracle, and a little ghostly.

When she first walked up I made a preliminary guess that her age is about fifty-five but the story she told showed she is older by several years because she remembered the Christmas of 1938.

She said until last Friday afternoon she had not given much thought to Christmas because she believed she had cancer and was dying. She had developed symptoms that seemed serious indeed and had gone through a flock of tests and the more tests she got the worse she felt and she thought, "This is what dying feels like."

The worst part was—she smiled and warned that the story would sound like a soap opera—the worst part was she thought she would die and her daughter wouldn't know she was gone. On account of some kind of family unhappiness she and the daughter had split and the two had not communicated for almost two years.

Then last Friday two things happened and I know you can guess what they were. First, all those tests she took came back negative, showing she didn't have cancer at all, and she began feeling a lot better. And kept feeling better until she got onto some kind of high and she couldn't stop smiling. Second thing was, the daughter called and guess where she was—out at Hobby Airport, just back from wherever she'd been, and asking if she could come home for Christmas.

The woman said those two happenings were almost more than she could stand. Said she felt like she had gone ahead and died, but had come back to life. She charged out and began getting ready for Christmas, and that's when the strange thing happened.

It was raining, and she was walking across a Northwest Mall parking lot and suddenly she began singing.

She stopped, and stood under that umbrella and sang this simple little song she had not heard or thought of in fifty years and yet she knew all the words and held the melody just right. She said, "It was a song my mother sang when I was a girl. Not a Christmas song especially. More like Thanksgiving."

Then she talked about the last time she remembered hearing that song. Christmas of '38. Her father was out of work, a common circumstance of those times. Then a week before

Christmas he got temporary work at a warehouse. He didn't get paid until late Christmas Eve.

"My mother went to the warehouse Christmas Eve and waited," the woman said. "Dad got paid about eight-thirty that night. Ten dollars. Together they went around in a hurry, before the stores closed, and bought us all presents, and if it hadn't been for that ten dollars we wouldn't have had any Christmas."

The singing of the song by the mother came the next morning, when they had ten dollars worth of presents all around them and that was a pretty good lot of presents because the average cost was something like fifty cents each. And before they began opening the gifts, the mother of the woman I met in the bank sang that song. Expressing thanks, for family and love and good fortune.

I have to admit, up to that point I wasn't much impressed by the story because it seemed a little too wet, as they say now, but the song interested me. I asked the woman to sing it for me.

She said, "That's the strange part. I can't sing it again. I can't quite get the tune. I know what the words say, but I can't call them up again."

So I asked how she could have sung the song in the parking lot and she said, "I don't believe that was me singing. I think it was my mother." ❧

145

City Boy

For a couple of years my friend Mel has been threatening to pay me a visit up here in Washington County. Kept saying he wanted to find out what was so much fun about sitting on the front porch of an old country house.

So finally he came, and spent the night. I was glad to have the company because I've been here a few days alone while my partner is up in New York, spending money.

Now Mel is one of your true urban dwellers, and has never had any hankering whatever for rural living. But he arrived in good form and made a couple of favorable comments about the old place. I walked him around and showed things.

When I was telling him about the big honeysuckle I transplanted from the woods to the yard, a bee zipped out of that vine and stung him on the side of the neck. Popped him good.

Funny thing, just the day before I had my head stuck in that honeysuckle vine for an hour while I was pulling weeds, and the bees on those blooms paid me no attention at all. And here's Mel standing ten feet away and he gets stung.

Half an hour later we were down on the creek back of the house and he got into fire ants. Something you don't do in fire ant country is go outdoors and stand still, without looking down to see what's at your feet. Mel had one shoe square in the middle of a fire ant mound and it didn't take those vicious scamps ten seconds to send an attack force up his britches leg and start stinging.

We had to come back to the house so he could take his pants off and clean the ants out. He counted a dozen stings.

Before sunset I took him berry picking. I thought it'd be nice if he could go home with a quart of dewberries, but he didn't enjoy picking. The briars kept gouging him, and he worried all the time about reaching down and touching a snake. Every crooked stick on the place looked like a snake to him.

Back on the porch we sat and waited for sunset and he said, "My Lord, what's that?"

I had to ask what he meant and he said, "That awful noise. Sounds like a lion or something."

Oh. That was my neighbor's bull. Sometimes a bull will walk around and make these deep sounds in his throat, not exactly a roar or a bellow or a grunt or a growl but having a hint of all those. Just a bull, talking about being a bull.

"What's that?" Mel asked five minutes after the bull got quiet. "Sounds like somebody in distress."

Well, it was a bird. A rain crow, or yellow-billed cuckoo. We've got several of those around here, and one of their calls is a series of low moaning notes. I've always loved that sound and it never occurred to me it could seem distressful.

We didn't sit on the porch long because the mosquitoes bothered Mel and I didn't have any repellent. So I took him in and fed him early.

For supper I'd fixed a one-dish meal, a pot of vegetables with nice hunks of chicken meat and I thought it was good. Mel said it wasn't bad but needed salt, and he sort of picked at it. I thought he wasn't feeling well.

So I started worrying about him a little. Those dozen fire

ant pops on top of a bee sting, would that be enough to give him a dangerous reaction?

But for dessert I had Blue Bell and he ate two big bowls and seemed to feel better because he asked if the Astro game would be on TV. I think it was but we don't have a TV up here. I could tell he thought that was truly strange, something like having a house without a roof.

I found the Astro game on the radio and we listened to a couple of innings. Mel kept watching the radio, as if it might develop a screen and produce a picture.

When we bought this old house we raised the roof and made an upstairs bedroom of the attic. I steered Mel to bed up there but I don't think he ever went to sleep. I kept hearing him stomp around, and he never turned off the light.

About two a.m. he came down and finished the night on the sofa. Said that upstairs room was full of rats, and had wasps in it, too.

Actually they're just mice, not really rats, and they almost never come out of the walls. But wasps, we do have wasps sometimes. I don't much blame him for not wanting to sleep with wasps after he's already been stung thirteen times.

Next morning he left early. Said he had a lot to do back in town. ❧

Sophie's Gift

"The first Christmas I remember," Madame Z was saying, "I must have been seven or eight years old. I don't know where I was, but I was staying with some people that had a girl named Sophie, with yellow hair. She gave me the first Christmas present I ever got."

I had gone down in the Brazos River Bottom to pay the December visit on my retired fortune-teller friend, and to take her a Christmas gift—a pair of wild red and yellow earrings in the shape of butterflies.

Big butterflies, too. Madame loves earrings, the bigger and flashier the better. The year before last, I think it was, I took her a pair with miniature bells that went tinkle, tinkle when she moved her head, and those were a great success.

She must have a bushel basket of ear decorations somewhere in her house because I've never seen her wearing the same ones twice. I expect I've given her earrings on at least a dozen Christmases and she always seems perfectly pleased. As if they were the very thing she dreamed of receiving. As if they came out of the most expensive jewelry store in town, which they surely did not.

When I go into the Bottom for the December call, my hope is that the spirit of the season will move my old friend to tell me a story out of her fertile past. That's why I asked what she remembered about her first Christmas, and got the surprising information that the first she remembered was when she was seven or eight years old.

Madame's earliest times have always been misty in her recollection. Either that, or she simply doesn't care to talk about the matter.

Some of the regular customers ask about Madame's age. She claims she doesn't know. She claims also not to recall a mother or a father or any early family life. She was passed around, as she calls it, and sometimes stayed here, and sometimes there.

But I've established that until she was old enough to get by on her own, and "go on down the road" as she says, she stayed on various Brazos Bottom plantations, scattered upstream and down, from just below Waco almost to the mouth of the river.

Madame tells me this was once a pattern along the Brazos: Orphan children "stayed" on farms where they were needed, to do chores and help in the kitchen and often in the fields, and when they weren't needed any longer they were passed along to other farms.

"That Sophie girl was about my same age," Madame said, holding the butterfly earrings up, watching as they turned and caught the light, "or at least my same size. I don't recall the name of those folks. I never was much on names, at least not last ones."

She paused to shine one of the earrings on her sleeve, and I asked why she didn't remember Christmas before she was eight. How about when she was three, and four, and five, along in there when Christmas is the most exciting for little children?

She shrugged. "I reckon it was because the people I was with then didn't have Christmas, or if they did I wasn't in on it. At Sophie's house that time I was working in the kitchen, and saw their stuff, their Christmas tree and all. I don't think I ever saw a Christmas tree before that, with the tinfoil and the star and so forth."

So, was she included in the celebration that went on in that home?

"Well, not exactly," Madame said. "Sophie, she was a pretty nice girl. Used to come back in the kitchen and talk to me while I was washing dishes. Dishes, Lordy. I washed so many dishes in big houses like that, I still dream about 'em, mountains of dirty dishes high as the ceiling. Reason I don't cook much right now, it makes such a mess to clean up. Anyway, I always thought Sophie was lonesome, without any sisters or brothers. Christmas afternoon she came and asked if I wanted to see the presents she got.

"We went to her room, and it was just a jungle of presents. Dolls, and clothes, and games, and a new bicycle, and a scooter, and every kind of toy you could name. Sophie asked me what all I got for Christmas and I told her I got nothing, and she said, 'Well, here, take one of my presents. You can pick out anything you want.' I took a pair of shoes."

Shoes? Why?

"I guess," she said, "it was because I didn't have any."

Ah. I agreed she made a good selection then.

"Oh, I don't know. I had days afterward, when I was going down the road afoot, I wished I'd picked the bicycle instead. Thanks for the earrings, and you have a merry merry." ❧

Delicious Toothpaste

*L*ast weekend I was searching for something I thought was hidden in my old carpenter's chest, which I use as a combination coffee table and trunk, and I ran across the Quote Book file.

I kept the Quote Book file for a good many years. When I heard somebody say something I thought was worth remembering, I wrote it out and stuck it in that file. I intended to collect about a bushel basketful of those quotations, and then when I got old and didn't have anything better to do, I meant to put them together into a book. I called it the Quote Book, which would be a bad title, but never mind because nobody would publish such a book anyhow, and even if it got published nobody would buy it.

But I enjoyed reading some of the quotations again. Like this one from Pappy Crate, who was living out in the Hill Country at Hunt when I met him. In '72 he was eighty-three and he said, "I quit smoking last spring because it was getting hard on my wind."

About the same time, I had a visit with Lena Killough Jackson, an elderly widow living alone and managing the Killough Ranch up near Hearne. I wondered if she ever got scared out there in that lonesomeness and she said, "No, I've got a forty-five pistol and seven bitin' dogs."

Then I liked what John Sturrock told me, when we were talking about how close to home East Texas country folks used to stay. In the early part of this century, some people in those woods would live out their lives and never travel more than fifty miles from where they were born.

Sturrock was talking about Eli Ballard, one of his neighbors long ago. Ballard was taken away from his home for the first time and rode in a wagon twenty-one miles west. When he got back he reported, "If the world's as big east as it is west, she's shore a gol'derner."

Another time I was up at Huffman on the Hargraves Ranch, drinking coffee with Willie Hargraves. The doorbell rang and I looked out and saw a horse standing on the front porch. Willie told me, "He always rings the bell when he wants his dinner." Then he went out and fed the horse.

Rural people, in my experience, give you far more startling information than city folks. One day C.A. Jackson in Highlands was talking about his country school days up in Bell County, back in Depression times. The county school superintendent was trying to encourage youngsters to brush their teeth and sample tubes of toothpaste were passed out in schools.

"That was the first toothpaste I ever saw," Jackson told me, "and it tasted better than anything I was getting then, so I ate it."

As far as I could tell, that's the truth. But I do know a lot of rural folks enjoy telling outrageous stories about hard times in the country.

Like Turkey Gates down at Wadsworth, below Bay City on the coast prairie. I used to keep up with Turkey mainly to see what he would say next, and I have several of his little tales in the Quote Book file.

Here's a sample: "During the Depression my daddy would

let a neighbor family have a ham hock to cook with their black-eyed peas, but it was just a loan and they had to bring it back when the peas were done."

Every page or so in this file I find a quotation that's not attributed to anybody, so I must have just heard such remarks in a crowd somewhere and didn't know who said them. A sample:

"When he was a boy about ten he was almost drowned in the Brazos River and all the rest of his life he wouldn't take anything but sponge baths, and he joined the Methodists instead of the Baptists because he couldn't stand to get in the water."

I find John Henry Key of Liberty County in my Quote Book file. I wrote down something he said about pork. It has the term "mast" in it, or simply "mass" as it's sometimes pronounced. To East Texans who hunt and eat wild hogs, mast is anything that drops off a tree and is eaten by razorbacks. Pecans, acorns, whatever falls. Here's the sentence I saved out of what I heard John Henry Key say:

"The best pork you can get is about a two-year-old razorback hog that'll weigh between a hundred and a hundred fifty pounds, killed when the mast has been good and you can taste the pecans in the bacon."

In that Big Thicket part of the state I also got a quote from an old-time fiddler named Savan Caruthers at Hull. He talked about the first time he ever came to town, out of the Thicket. He was seven years old and could already play the fiddle. Listen to this, which is one of the most extraordinary quotes I ever collected:

"My daddy brought me into Batson, to a saloon. I was scared and wanted to run away but they tied my leg to a table and made me play, and the men would pitch me coins."   ∾

Sitting Ducks Beware

At the afternoon coffee hour I sat and listened to a fellow talk about teaching his son to hunt birds, and I was reminded of the only bird-hunting lesson I ever had. My cousin Maurice Willet was the teacher.

This was up in Palo Pinto County, west of Fort Worth, back in Depression times when members of our family shot birds for only one reason, and that was to eat them. Our men weren't sports hunters in any way.

The young father I heard at the drugstore spoke of teaching his son how to lead a bird in flight. I'm glad he didn't witness that lesson I got from Cousin Maurice, who did not believe in shooting at birds while they were flying. They were way too hard to hit in the air.

Shotgun shells sold then two for a nickel and this was a significant amount. Cousin Maurice lectured on the value of nickels. One of his examples was that a nickel would buy a sack of Bull Durham smoking tobacco, with a book of cigarette papers. So if you fired both barrels of a twelve-gauge shotgun without hitting anything, it was the same as wasting an entire sack of Bull Durham. Furthermore, in Fort Worth then, if you went to the right store you could buy a quart of milk for a nickel. Or if you wanted to spend it on a luxury, you could go to the candy store and buy a peanut patty pretty near as big as a dinner plate.

Anyhow, for the hunting lesson we went to the stock tank and hid behind some oak shinnery. We kept still and waited for the doves to come in for water.

The idea, as Cousin Maurice demonstrated, was to get two or three doves lined up at the edge of the water so you could kill at least a pair with one shot. If you shot and killed only one bird, you were wasteful. Cousin Maurice did not consider one dove to be worth an entire shotgun shell. On a dove hunt he might shoot only three times, and go home with six birds.

Shooting doves on the ground that way would get a primal scream out of a present-day sportsman, but that was how we did it, without any thought that it was not sporting.

In my high school years I went on a quail hunt or two, mainly as an observer because there would be four or five boys and only one shotgun. The method of hunting was to find a covey of birds and blast into them, on the ground, and see how many you could get with one shot. I don't remember doing that myself but I watched it done, and I would have done it if I had ever gotten a turn with the gun.

We hunted ducks the same way cousin Maurice hunted doves. We'd slip up on a tank and hope to find two or three ducks in a row. On the water, of course. Blam. Then risk pneumonia by wading out and picking up whatever we hit.

Dogs? Oh sure, we had dogs but they weren't any good for retrieving. They'd chase rabbits and tree possums and booger bark at strangers but if one of those mutts ever got a duck in his mouth he'd run out in the brush and hide and eat it.

Understand I am not trying to defend that kind of hunting. I am just telling you, this is how we did it.

When I left that old poor country and went in the Army,

they sent me to aerial gunnery school. First thing they did at that school was put me out on a skeet range, to shoot at clay pigeons with a twelve-gauge shotgun.

Well, as a graduate of Cousin Maurice Willet's stationary target school of shooting, naturally I couldn't hit a clay pigeon in flight. After I'd missed about half a dozen times this sergeant came up and asked, "Where you from, soldier?" Told him I was from Texas and he said, "Well, you lead these pigeons just like those Texas ducks. Didn't you ever shoot ducks?" I thought a few seconds and decided not to tell him about the way we shot ducks where I came from. Probably he'd think I was smarting off and I'd end up on KP.

Besides, in civilian life he was bound to be one of those dedicated sportsmen out of Nebraska or somewhere. He had the leathery face and the steely eyes I'd seen in Field and Stream pictures, of guys with shotguns cradled in their arms, and spotted bird dogs alongside, and the feathers of dead pheasants poking out of their jackets. A fellow like that, you don't even want to hint to him that you ever shot a duck sitting on the water.

One of this life's ironies is that I went through a genuine shooting war as a gunner, and we won anyway. ❧

His War's Never Over

$\mathcal{E}$very year when the calendar reminds me about V-E Day, I see that kid's face again.

He had fallen, trying to negotiate one of the intricate turns and tricky steps and low overheads that make a big ship hard to get around in for landlubbers, even when they're healthy and have all their parts still attached and operating.

This kid was missing a leg, above the knee, and part of an arm as well, and even after fifty years I can see the redness of the fresh scar on the side of his face. A ragged pattern. Looked like the kind of mess a chunk of flak might make.

A lot of guys were moving around the ship that day, pausing sometimes to join in small groups and talk and smoke and nod or shake their heads. The news had just come in. The ship was the SS *Mariposa* and we were in the middle of the Atlantic, coming home. We'd left out of Naples and were headed for Boston and the captain had come on the squawk system with the announcement that the war in Europe was over.

Maybe there was some sort of shouting when the word came but I don't remember it. I do remember a low buzz of voices shortly after the announcement. But no smiles. No handshaking or back slapping. Certainly no laughter. No celebration.

The guys returning home on that ship had already fought their war. They'd flown their missions over Europe in the heavy bombers like the B-17s and 24s and the mediums like the B-25s and the fighters like the P-51s and 38s. Or they'd endured Sicily in ground troops, and survived landings at awful places like Anzio, and fought across North Africa before that.

A great majority of us on that vessel would never see a shooting war again. A few would be sent on to the Pacific, and some would stay in the military as career people and see action in Korea, and even Vietnam. But most of us were through with war forever and we sensed it and it's reasonable to suppose that we would celebrate the end of the war in Europe.

I think to this day that we did not celebrate because we had on board with us a lot of young men whose war would never be over.

They were the wounded, repaired just enough to travel. Hundreds of them, quiet guys with solemn eyes and grim mouths, many still in bandages. We walked among them daily and they reminded us silently that you can say a war is over, and you can make a dramatic announcement about its being over, and celebrate its being over, but it's not, not ever.

That's the main thing I learned from being in a war.

I have tried to decide the age of the kid who fell that day. He looked so young. I was twenty-three then, and felt years older than he looked. He seemed like eighteen. Probably he was twenty-one.

He wasn't my buddy. I'd not seen him before. I just happened along a passageway at the time one of his crutches skidded when he was trying to get around a corner, and he went down, and hard.

A couple of other guys were with me when the kid fell. We jumped to his side to help him, and one of us touched his good arm to start lifting and he jerked it away and he spit the word with such fierceness. "No!"

Meaning that he didn't want any help getting up, that he would get up by himself, and the expression on his round face is still a photograph in my head. A combination of bitterness and anger and pain and determination.

He did get up alone and go on along the passageway, and I never saw him again but I've thought of him so many times. When we celebrate victories in wars, and observe the anniversaries of the ending of wars, I automatically retrieve the image of that young guy's face, looking up at us and saying that one word with such ferocity.

On that day, the news about the war was spreading across the world and people were spilling out into streets and shouting and hugging one another. Or going to church and sinking to their knees to give thanks. Or bulging into bars to get drunk, in celebration of victory.

And here's this young guy clodding along on his crutches, on a ship going home. Home to what? To more war.

The war for him has never ended, not in half a century, nor for any of the other thousands like him, unless they are dead. ∽

Normandy

*I*n May of 1994 the Chronicle *sent me to France to write about the fiftieth anniversary of the Normandy Invasion. I got that juicy assignment because I've had so many birthdays. I'm the oldest member of the paper's editorial staff. And I was stationed in Europe, though not in France, when that invasion came to pass in 1944.*

On the journey to Normandy my partner went along. She manages French pretty well, and since we sometimes strayed far off the tourist trails, without her I doubt I'd ever have found Normandy, or done what I went over there to do.

We began in England. The reason was, we had this Plan. We thought it would be appropriate to follow the general path that American troops took on the way to the Invasion. Go to England first, then cross the English Channel, enter France at Cherbourg, visit the beaches where the landing was made, then roam through Normandy's bocage *and the small towns where so much of the fighting took place. And finally to Paris, and back home.*

We sent back a dozen stories, first from England and then France. The following section has been compiled from them:

HIGHCLIFFE, Dorset—A wet gray day here on the south coast of England, where we've found a shelter in a grassy park on a bluff overlooking Christchurch Bay. Light rain is coming out of a low cloud cover that's beginning to seem friendly. It has hung over us most of the time we've been in England.

The orderly little town of Highcliffe is just behind us. I can look a mile left and another right, along clean beaches. The Isle of Wight and the cities of Southampton and Portsmouth are nearby to the east. Bournemouth to the west.

My map says the water at the foot of this cliff is Christchurch Bay but a short way offshore it becomes the English Channel. Which looks calm from here but the surf breaking below talks about open sea and broad swells. Tall sails materialize out in the mist. Awkward surfers laugh and splash in the rain.

If I could look seventy-five miles south across the channel I would see Cherbourg, at the top of Cotentin Peninsula in Normandy.

Now let's flip back through the calendars to a day similar to this, in late May of 1944. The park may not have been here then but the cliff was, and visitors came to sit and look out to sea. I'm certain of that. People are drawn to high places on seashores.

An American soldier was here that day, half a century ago. I can see him, sitting here near me, his legs drawn up a bit, arms hooked over knees. Perfectly still. Staring out across the channel.

He knows.

He doesn't yet know when but he knows that soon he'll be on a transport out there in the channel and near the other side he'll load onto a landing craft and he'll have to walk down the ramp and into the surf and face enemy fire, somewhere over there on the coast of the continent.

He's a private, probably with the 4th Infantry Division. I'm guessing he's nineteen, maybe twenty. From San Marcos. Or from Scranton, or Brooklyn, or Phoenix. He and hundreds of thousands of others have been here long enough to know that the invasion of Europe is certain to begin this spring.

Everybody knows. The Germans know. British

school children know, since all the south of England seems about to sink into the sea from the weight of trucks and tanks and guns and tents and troops and mountains of supplies and ammunition. How could anybody not know?

Do you imagine this young soldier here on the cliff is angry at Germans and eager to get across the channel and into the war? No. I can tell you what he's feeling, because I've felt it.

There's a lurking emptiness in him, in his chest and gut. It's the fear of this thing to come, this awfulness that can end his life, or ruin it. Fear not just of dying but of horrors that are known but aren't talked about in the tents. Getting the legs blown off. Being blinded. Catching one in the belly and lying on the beach all day, waiting to die. Or falling in the sea on the transfer to the landing craft and, weighed by all that equipment, going down like a stone.

Doubt, too, is a part of the emptiness. A feeling of weakness. Gnawing questions. Can he do this? Can he face the fire and fight, or will he cower and fall and cry? Because in battle some men do.

He is not really prepared. Not so many months ago he was playing ball in a school yard. He may not be able to kill. He has never seen a person killed.

He hasn't yet heard the code name Omaha Beach, where he will wade ashore next week, on June sixth.

I watch him draw a deep breath now, blow it out, rise, dust off the seat of his pants, and leave for wherever his outfit waits.

≈

From England we took a huge comfortable ferry across the Channel to Cherbourg and the main thing I recall now about that crossing is the children.

When we took on this assignment, trying to trace the path our troops took on the way to the Invasion, we didn't know about the children. In the spring, multitudes of school children are on group tours all over that part of the world.

The first day of the trip, when we got to London, the airport was overrun with them. Hundreds of squiggling children, some not yet a yard tall. I thought that was nice, all those kiddos getting out of school to visit the airport.

Next morning I went to watch the changing of the guard at Buckingham Palace and the children were there, too, and their adults along with them and they were all speaking what to me was foreign language.

I went over in St. James' Park and spent two hours and never heard a word of English, there in that splendid green London place, with ducks and swans and ponds and great trees. And children, everywhere, acres of them, and they were Italian, German, French, Asian, and no telling what other kinds there might have been. But not English, not one English child. I suppose all the English youngsters were off on spring tours of their own, to other countries.

When we boarded the ferry the children were still with us, going to France. I felt we were oversupplied with them so we escaped by taking seats in an adults-only section where waiters brought refreshments and food. The idea of following the troop trail to Normandy was beginning to look a little far-fetched. Imagine infantrymen, on their way to a combat landing, being served cold beer and sandwiches by white-shirted waiters. And all those children on board. We abandoned the Plan.

Looking back at them now, I am impressed by those young-sters. They were chattery and giggly but generally well be-haved. They were forever eating junk food the way American kids do but I never once saw any of them tossing their wrap-pings on the deck or overboard into the channel. Pretty nice people.

Here's part of a story we sent home after our first day in Normandy:

THROUGH THE *BOCAGE*—Rolling down N-13 in a rented Peugeot, a diesel stick shift with five forward speeds, plus a reverse if you can find it.

So we're out of England and into France. This high-way drops out of Cherbourg and runs south and east into the green country called Lower Normandy. Through towns whose names will stir memories for white-haired guys who fought here fifty years ago. Valognes. Sainte Mère-Église. Carentan. Bayeux.

We're pointing for Port-en-Bessin, where I hope they're holding a hotel room for us because this north-ern coast of France is filling fast with visitors, busloads of them, on their way to anniversary doings. Already we've met up with groups from New York, California, Illinois.

Bocage. Pronounce it something like boh-CAHGE. It's the name for the type of landscape common in this region. We're running through *bocage* now. Small flat fields and pastures bordered by elevated hedgerows. Often cut by narrow one-horse lanes. Accompanied by stone farm houses and Holstein cows. Neat little vil-lages every few miles.

Tourists from wherever, riding those big chartered

buses, have the advantage that they can see over the hedgerows from their elevated seats. American tank commanders in '44 hated *bocage* because they couldn't see over the hedges, couldn't see anything except what was directly ahead in the narrow roads, and they often ran into enemy resistance before they knew it was near.

Accounts of the Battle of Normandy are peppered with fierce comments from officers and men about *bocage.* Easy country to defend. But hell to attack . . .

The next few days we walked along the north shore beaches where the Invasion took place. There were five landing points that June day in '44, along fifty-six miles of Normandy coast. American forces came in at Omaha and at Utah. British and Canadian troops at Gold, Juno and Sword beaches.

OMAHA BEACH — Another gray day on the north coast of France. The surf gentle, the English Channel tide at its low point. I'm standing at the vegetation line, looking out over the beach, and I'm surprised by the width of it.

A while ago I walked out to the water, a pretty good hike over the wet sand. I'm guessing the beach at this point is five hundred yards wide, maybe more.

Behind me the green shore rises sharply. It's not a cliff, not along here. Cliffs of major-league kinds do rise on this coast to the west but right here the land comes out of the sea on what I would call just a good deep-breathing uphill climb. Still, a mighty nasty ascent, considering all those guns blasting down at the climbers.

In addition to the breadth of this beach, there are other surprises. I didn't imagine I would ever have such a thought about Omaha Beach but I have to say that it's beautiful. So smooth and pink and clean. I almost said peaceful.

Near me a young mother strolls, carrying her tiny baby. She watches a fellow about her age speed along the beach on a wheeled surfboard, rigged with a sail. Off to my left about a dozen schoolboys fool around, splashing in tidal pools. Tripping one another. Throwing shells.

Do you suppose these young people understand what happened here fifty years ago? Surely they do. A couple of monuments are in sight, up at the top of the green slope, and their inscriptions tell part of the story. But half a century is forever to the young and maybe now this beach is simply a pleasant place to play.

Coastal towns just inland from here are Colleville, St. Laurent, Les Moulins, Vierville, Le Grand Hameau —names unforgettable to American soldiers who survived this Omaha landing. Those are places where their friends died, where they themselves came close.

The record I've read says Omaha was a nightmare, a blood bath, the toughest of all the landings made on D-Day. Invading Normandy required a great deal more than foot soldiers wading onto beaches but I've always felt the worst job belonged to the guys who had to walk ashore here that morning in '44 under such heavy enemy fire.

That might be wrong. The worst assignment might have belonged to the paratroops who had to go in first and jump at night behind enemy lines, and some landed square in the nests of German soldiers. Or the worst job might have gone to the company of Rangers who climbed the cliff a few mile west of here at Pointe-du-Hoc, going after a battery of German artillery.

But whatever the toughest job was, the Invasion has always been symbolized for me by combat soldiers coming off those landing craft.

Earlier this day I was at the top of the rise where German concrete bunkers still sit, solid as stone mountains. I went in one of the bunkers and played a little war game, the way young boys do. I became a German soldier in there, an artillery man or a machine gunner or a rifleman. I was there the morning of June 6, 1944 and I saw the landing craft moving in, out of the mist, and stopping, and I watched their ramps drop, and out poured American soldiers, awkward and stumbling in water to their waists, overloaded with equipment, and shooting down on them was easy and killing them was easy and I couldn't understand why. Why did they keep coming out of those strange boats to be killed?

But of course we know the answer. They kept coming because they had no choice.

Being here, looking out over the beach where they came in, and where so many died before they reached the bottom of the slope, I feel no sense of victory about the Invasion. I feel only grief.

∾

Our second day on the Normandy beaches we were at Pointe-du-Hoc, looking out to sea from the brink of the cliffs, and a young fellow about thirty, an American attending the anniversary observance, came up and asked me, "Were you here then?"

I was asked that question several times, due to my gray hair and wrinkles. All elderly men visiting those beaches during that anniversary time were given particular respect, just in case they were veterans of the Invasion. Young people stepped aside to let them pass. Walk up to a chattering group and the chatter would cease.

No, I wasn't anywhere near Normandy in '44. I was in a war, but a different kind.

I was over in Italy, living in a tent and eating three meals a day and going to town now and then on overnight passes. Three, sometimes four days a week I'd get on a Fifteenth Air Force B-24 and sit behind a pair of fifty-caliber machine guns and we'd fly across the Adriatic and drop five hundred-pound bombs on places like Vienna and Munich.

The Germans would shoot at us and sometimes they'd hit us and I saw friends die, but not at close range. I never watched buddies die beside me, the way foot soldiers did.

We didn't fly every day. Some days we lay on our butts and wrote letters and read dog-eared paperbacks and at six o'clock we slogged up to the day-room and drank bad cherry brandy and waited for chow.

One thing we did every day, we went to headquarters and studied the big map they kept on the wall. Daily they changed the lines on the map, showing progress ground forces had made toward Berlin, moving toward the end of the war.

That's what we were most interested in—the end of it, so we could go home. And we understood that we wouldn't end it by dropping bombs from airplanes flying four miles high. It would have to be done by the ground troops who caused the lines to move on that map.

If I had to be in another war, I would want to do it that same way, in the air. I don't much like airplanes and especially not when they're being shot at, but they make a good way to fight wars. As opposed to carrying rifles and walking onto enemy beaches.

We used to bitch about getting waked up early. I'm talking about a guy coming in your tent at three a.m. and kicking your cot and telling you your name was on the list so roll out and enjoy your breakfast.

You did get a pretty fair breakfast and then you flew across the Adriatic and did a mission on Germany or Austria, usually on railroad yards or oil refineries. And if you didn't get hit by anti-aircraft fire, in about six or seven hours you were home again and you'd go to your tent and stretch out, or have a hot shower before chow.

While you rested you made another mark in your letter-writing kit, or wherever you kept the record on the number of missions you'd flown. And when you reached a certain total, they sent you home. Where I was, the magic number was fifty.

Even then, when we wrote to our girlfriends about how we were winning the war, we knew who was doing the fighting that counted the most—those dogfaces down in the shell holes and mud, the men whose names are on the white crosses in the military graveyards in France.

NORMANDY AMERICAN CEMETERY—What you do, after you've come all this way, and seen what there is to see and hear what there is to hear, you end up asking whether the Normandy Invasion was worth the awful price.

Maybe it's a question that shouldn't be asked, since there's no satisfactory answer. But you ask it all the same, and the place where the question begs an answer strongest is in the Normandy American Cemetery.

Names of the men who paid for what we call a victory are engraved on the white crosses and on the six-pointed stars.

. . . William J. Stewart . . . Perry H. Hamilton . . . Dolph J. Lackey . . . Calvin C. Postma . . . Samuel B. Shapiro . . . Claude H. Reynolds . . . John H. Shepard . . . Travis L. Hughes . . . August P. Tellenni . . . Francis Walsh . . . Robert Gerth . . . Lewis Chapman . . .

The cemetery is a beautiful place, maintained in a state of perfection. You've seen the pictures in the paper and on TV, the crosses and stars in those precise rows, the grass clipped like golf greens. The land was given by the French, but your federal taxes pay for the up-keep.

More than 9,000 of our dead are buried here. Most were killed during the landings along this coast. Close to 3,000 died on D-Day. Many of those are not in this cemetery because they were taken home for burial. But 3,000 dead, in one day, in a battle that we won? Say that number fast and there's not much pain or sadness in it.

Three thousand, three thousand. Do you ever wonder who they were?

. . . Robert A. Morgan . . . Glenden Dennis . . . Salvatore S. Arnone . . . Kail Frank . . . Clifford Voss . . . Henri E. Cleabanne . . . Arthur Sylvia . . . William Smedegar . . . Kenneth R. Baum . . . Michael S. Oreschak . . . Clyde E. Baker . . . Robert E. Featherstone . . . James B. Alcorn . . . Theodore Dickter . . . Charles Billings . . .

It's hard to argue that the campaign was anything but a high accomplishment. The idea of it is staggering. A million military people involved. An armada of something like 7,000 vessels. Close to 10,000 airplanes. Never been anything like it, in all the centuries that people have been fighting and killing one another.

So the Invasion was a success, despite that so much went wrong, so many lives lost and mistakes made. Navigation errors. Judgment errors. Incredible heroics in some places, the opposite in others. But when entire Allied outfits were slaughtered, others came in to take their places, and they kept on coming, and coming, and eventually Normandy was liberated, and Paris, and Berlin fell, and Hitler died, and the war in Europe was over.

Maybe it's true, like they say, that this was the last good war. We were all in support of it, and we saved the culture of Europe and defeated the evil that threatened us. So is it reasonable to say that the price was too high? The answer would need to come from those we can't ask.

. . . James D. Johnston . . . Henry G. Bohlen . . . Casimir J. Stuczynski . . . Peter J. Yalch . . . Loy Thorne . . . Joseph T. Finnegan . . . Robert P. Noble . . . Smith G. Griffin Jr. . . . Wilmer W. Bailly . . . Clyde E. Baker . . . John R. Ray . . . Edward H. Bostick . . . Henry C. Mitchell . . . Donald A. Gillie . . . Karl K. Hicks . . . Nathan Nissenson . . . Ollie M. Denton . . .

A fair number of intelligent people thought the Invasion was a mistake, that we should have kept dropping bombs on Hitler's troops, forced them to surrender before we sent in ground forces from the west.

Maybe the airplane people were right. Maybe if we'd held off on the Invasion we'd have ended up dropping The Bomb on Berlin instead of Japan and the world would be different now.

But there's also the argument that German scientists might have had time to develop The Bomb for Hitler. If that had happened, I might not be here to write this sentence, and you probably wouldn't be here to read it. There's no way to know, for certain, what the names on the crosses and stars mean to us now, and maybe that's the saddest thing of all.

. . . Walter H. Paige, Jr. . . . John Hanriot . . . Edward Campbell . . . Arnold Schinkoeth . . . Richard Weiser . . . Ira Davis . . . Donald J. Mallard . . . Walse H. Dunbar . . . Paul E. Owens . . . James Harrelson . . . William Solomon . . . Lon Civitarese . . . Sam Monceaux . . . Lawrence E. Jackson . . .

∽

When we got home a friend asked me if I enjoyed going to Normandy.

No, I hated it. There were things about the overall trip that I enjoyed. I loved London and England and a couple of days in Paris on the way home were great. I'll remember some excellent meals in an old hotel at Port-en-Bessin and coastal Normandy is pretty country. But the reason for the visit made it impossible to enjoy. How are you going to enjoy going to a pretty land when it reminds you constantly of death? War and killing and death.

The friend said to me, Come on, all that was fifty years ago. Not to me it wasn't. It was yesterday to me. All those thousands who died there, they were my bunch, my generation, and I hurt for them.

On those beaches I did fairly well until I began running across the U.S. military boys sent to Normandy to help with that D-Day observation. I watched them in the big cemetery at Omaha Beach, walking among the crosses and stars, reading the names, then pausing and looking out to sea with such solemn eyes. This got to me. I couldn't bear even to talk to those boys.

Look at them. Big and strong and smart and healthy and courteous. These are the kinds of youths killed in that Invasion, good people the world needs now, and there are things about the way they died that trouble me. It was too much like human sacrifice.

No, I'm glad I went to Normandy but I didn't enjoy it.

3.

A Nice Little Wedding

*L*ast weekend I went to a small wedding held in a home on Stanmore Drive. Pretty nice little ceremony, I thought.

I don't always enjoy weddings, and in fact as a rule I stay clear of them, because most are too much like funerals to suit me. All that dreary music, and the people looking so blamed solemn. The men always seem uncomfortable, as if their shirt collars are maybe a size too small, and half the women are apt to be crying. I've been to weddings where you could have hung some crepe and rolled in a casket and passed the entire enterprise off as a burying instead of a marrying.

But this ceremony on Stanmore Drive was sort of loose and casual. I doubt anybody shed tears. I did hear a good deal of giggling from the spectators, and at a critical point in the ritual, the bride and groom took time to get in what you might call a mild argument, about the rings getting mixed up. But evidently it wasn't a serious disagreement because they went ahead and got married.

I don't believe I ever saw a prettier bride. Dark eyes and hair, almost black, against a flawless creamy complexion. Also a sort of intelligent, aristocratic look that I can't describe, so I won't try. (I've always thought intelligent women were the most attractive.)

In a splendid blue dress and with orchids in her hair, she looked about thirty years old to me. But then there was her son standing beside her, to help his mama get married, and he's a junior in high school so she's got to be older than she looked.

My gang was there, too. My son, the happy nomad, all the way from Wisconsin or Kansas or wherever the invitation reached him. And my daughter and her husband from Galveston Island. What's going on here?

The groom? Well, he seemed a good many years older than the bride, if you ask me. And saying it that way is being polite. But these things happen nowadays.

The preacher came down from Amarillo to do this one wedding. He's David Horsley, who happens to be a friend of mine. Funny thing, long as I've known David I've never thought to ask him what brand of preacher he is. Like whether he's Methodist, Baptist, Lutheran, or whatever. But then on weddings I don't suppose it makes any difference.

David and his wife, Michele, lived here in Houston until just recently and one day they loaded up and moved to Amarillo. I don't know why. Maybe they need preachers up there worse than we do, but I doubt it.

Before that little wedding the house was full of guests, wandering around, waiting for time, and I got a chance to mingle and listen. I'm a licensed eavesdropper, and I think one of the most interesting things about weddings is what the guests say before the ceremony begins.

You hear stuff like, "I understand she wrote the ceremony herself, and gave it to the preacher and said, 'Here, read this.'"

Then the response. "I know. They tell me she rewrote the

wedding service in the Book of Common Prayer, and took out the part about promising to obey."

Also this:

"I'll bet he's twenty-five years older than she is if he's a day."

The response: "Well, she's been going around with him for seven years, so she ought to know what she's getting." (They had that one wrong. Actually it's nine years, not seven. I am in a position to know this is true.)

Then this comment about marriage ceremonies: "You come to a wedding now, you never know what you're going to hear. People are getting away from the traditional service."

Now that's gospel, in spades. I have lately studied a number of what you have to call wedding scripts (getting ready, you understand, to attend the event there on Stanmore), and some are truly startling. They run on for pages and pages, and the entire families of the bride and groom get involved in the vows, and all the members from both sides take oaths that they will support the marriage. When the preacher asks for responses, you've got fifty folks yelling, "We will! We will!"

I don't know about that. To me it sounds too much like marrying a family instead of a wife. I've had experience at marrying families, and it showed me that one wife at a time is plenty to handle.

But getting back to the little wedding on Stanmore, I thought everything came off fairly well, if you discount the mix-up about the rings. I was the one on the bride's right, where the groom stands. Afterward I felt really fine, and we all watched the Oilers beat the New Orleans Saints, 23-10. ❧

Call It Conversation

"Nothing's on TV," she said. "Let's cut it off." So off went the set, throwing the house into silence.

We sat still a little while. The ears need time to recover when you suddenly deprive them of racket. Presently we heard a tick-tick-ticking from the back of the house. What's that?

"It's the second hand on the kitchen clock."

Funny thing. I hadn't heard that before.

Then from the next room came the sort of sound I would describe as schloppy. Schlop, schlop, schlop. What's *that*?

"It's one of the dogs, licking her paw."

Time was eight p.m. Supper finished. Kitchen cleaned, or almost. We spent a few minutes thinking of what we might do if we weren't going to watch TV.

We could read. Or listen to music. Or go to a movie. Or rent a movie, say a good old bad one with John Wayne or Humphrey Bogart.

Or we could go see friends. Just show up without any notice, the way people used to do. Walk up and bang on the door and yell, "Hey, anybody home? You've got company." Did we really want to do that? Naw.

Or how about going riding, as we once called it? Sometimes we do that. Get in the car at night and roll around, see places

182

we seldom go. Downtown. Out to the Texas Medical Center. But it was raining. Can't see much on a rainy night.

Well, we could always go back to work. Might get a lot done from eight-thirty until eleven p.m. We took a vote and going back to work lost, 2 to 0.

"Hey," she said, "I know what let's do. Let's talk."

Talk?

"Yeah. It takes at least two people. You face one another, like this, and one says something and the other responds and you keep going, back and forth. It's called conversation."

Told her I wasn't sure I knew how to do that and she said:

"Let's try it, anyhow. You want to go first?"

No.

So she went first, and talked about houses, and about the kind of house she'd have if she could have exactly the one she wants, and where it would be.

She brought out a book she'd just read, "A Year In Provence," about a couple who went to southern France and took a house. I saw that's what she'd really like to do—go to France and live for a year, because she has relatives over there and speaks the language, at least somewhat.

I ended up confessing I've always wanted to try living a while in a foreign country, too, but I was thinking more in terms of New York, or Montana. If I had to fly across an ocean I would pick England, where I can almost understand what people are saying.

She said if I wanted England and she wanted France, no problem, we could work out a compromise, and go to France. Which was a joke but I heard the ring of truth in it.

I said I doubt the *Chronicle* would enjoy sending my paycheck to Europe, or New York, either, and I saw she was ready to drop the matter, but not for long.

We changed the subject to: Recycling. Country music. The

Persian Gulf mess. Guacamole salad. Snoring. Chocolate-covered cherries. Tractors and mowing machines. Raising children. I forget all the other topics. Must have been a dozen more.

This conversation—what a strange word—lasted three hours. I was amazed. It was educational.

I found out she hates chocolate-covered cherries. I love them, and always buy them at Christmas because in my early times, those curious little sweetish, drippy candies represented to me the very essence of the holiday season.

Also she doesn't like ham and cheese sandwiches, or what she calls "the plastic, make-believe kind of country music." But she loves George Jones, and Merle, and Willie, along with Mozart. And she loves the side of a hill in the country when frost has flattened native grasses and made them the color of winter. So it's all right.

These are things of value people need to know about one another, and about themselves. I found out that in social gatherings, I often sit in a corner and don't say more than two dozen words all night. Maybe I'll learn to talk. ∾

A Pretty Horse

Wwith Old Friend Morgan I was rolling down U.S. 77 below Kingsville, through the big ranches of South Texas. This is home country for O.F. In the forties he was a pipeline surveyor and walked hundreds of miles through that brushland.

When you're going south on 77, the Santa Gertrudis Division of the King Ranch lies to the right. O.F. was looking out at the mesquite and getting ready to tell a story. I have learned over the years to recognize the symptoms. He shifts his weight around, and wiggles his fingers, and sometimes raises his head like an old wolf sniffing the wind. This may go on for five, six miles, before the story starts coming out:

"In 1945," he began, waving to the west, "our survey party was working across this Santa Gertrudis Division here, and the King Ranch assigned these survey-sitters to go along with us.

"No survey party was allowed on the ranch without those sitters, as we called them. They were ranch hands who kept an eye on you, and saw that you didn't violate any rules. King Ranch always had rules.

"For instance, on the Santa Gertrudis they even had rules about driving stakes for the transit. In certain pastures they'd make us drive stakes flush with the ground, and that made it tough sometimes for the instrument man to locate his setups, and I thought it was a strange rule. But when the ranch had a rule, you observed it and didn't ask questions. We drove stakes flush.

"Anyhow, while we were working on the Santa Gertrudis I got acquainted with its foreman, Lauro Cavazos, and one evening after work he showed me the racehorse stables there at division headquarters. I got to see Bold Venture, the Kentucky Derby winner, and took a picture of him. I saw the entire thoroughbred setup, a real treat for me because I've always loved horses.

"That day Mr. Cavazos pointed out to me a beautiful two-year-old and said it was the reason for the rule about driving the transit stakes flush. They thought a lot of that horse and when he was a foal he was playing around and pawed a survey stake and hurt one of his forefeet. Mr. Cavazos said the horse probably would never race on account of that injury, but the ranch was keeping him around as a possible stud in their breeding program.

"Lauro Cavazos was an extraordinary fellow. He'd been on the King Ranch since 1912, and he'd even fought on it, and for it. In 1915 he was one of sixteen men who fought off fifty-eight Mexican bandits who'd come up from Matamoros and attacked the headquarters of the Norias Division. He fought in World War I, too, and came back and spent the rest of his life on this ranch. He's dead now.

"But you still hear about his children, his sons. One turned out to be the president of Texas Tech University, and then U.S. Secretary of Education. That was Lauro Cavazos Jr., the first Hispanic in the presidential Cabinet. Another son, Richard, became a four-star general. A third one, that was Bobby Cavazos, was the athlete and became a running back in pro football. All of them grew up here on this ranch.

"But I guess the thing I saw on Santa Gertrudis that turned

out to be the most special was that colt, that pretty horse with the crippled foot.

"The next year, in '46, a King Ranch entry won the Kentucky Derby, the Preakness, and the Belmont. The Triple Crown. His name was Assault, and he ran sort of funny because he had something the matter with one of his forefeet. The race writers called him the Three-Footed Wonder. The story was, Assault had hurt his foot when he was young, down here on the Santa Gertrudis.

"That gave me a big kick, because of the day Lauro Cavazos pointed out to me the colt with the hurt foot. He was the one that caused me and the survey crew to drive stakes flush with the ground, and he was Assault, the winner of the Triple Crown."   ❧

One Moment, Please

My friend Mel came by to visit and said: "The world has gotten so strange. Even going out to buy a lamp is strange."

I asked how buying a lamp was strange, and he told this story:

"Back in 1950 I was in a furniture store, right here in this town, and I saw a desk lamp I liked. Price on it was $24.50, which I thought was a little high, but I looked it over and it seemed all right. I told the clerk standing there that I wanted that lamp. He said fine, and I wrote him a check and took the lamp and went out.

"I kept that lamp on my desk forty-three years. It had a good heavy switch on it. That's where lamps go bad on you, their switches. Then one of my grandkids was roaming around the house the other morning, playing with a plastic sword, and he knocked my old lamp off the desk and broke the base.

"Well, I figured forty-three years was long enough for a lamp to last, so I went out to a furniture store, one of those big places, covers acres and acres, to see if I could find another lamp. I went in and there were three or four people waiting in a sort of lobby, and a nice-looking lady stepped out and asked what I was interested in, and I said lamps. She said, 'Come this way, please.'

"We walked I guess a block and a half before we got through all the rugs and living room suites and came to the lamps. Took me about half an hour, but finally I found a lamp that looked something like the one that got broken, and the price on it was $199.

"I thought that was high, but it seemed almost as good a lamp as I bought forty-three years ago for $24.50, so probably the price was about right. I told the lady I'd take it, and I got out my checkbook. She said: 'Just a moment, please. Let's see if the lamp is in stock.'

"She went over to a computer terminal and started tapping, and watching the screen, and tapping, and finally she said yes, the lamp was in stock. Which was not news to me because I had the thing in my hand. But then I saw the deal, that I wasn't going to get that particular lamp, but another one like it. The lady said, 'Come this way, please.'

"We walked another block and came to a place that looked like where they sold cars. You know those stalls, in car dealerships? Where people sit and look guilty and talk to a guy with three pencils in his shirt pocket? I hate stalls like that.

"But I figured it was just a place for me to write the check, so I sat down and began, but the lady came and sat across from me and had a form to fill out. Name, address, phone, things like that. Hey, I'm not applying for credit to pay out the lamp by the month. All I want to do is give 'em my check and get my lamp and go. She said, 'Just a moment, please.'

"She got up and went to another computer, and tapped on it, and tapped, and waited, and after a while she came back with a set of forms, and showed me where to sign them, in triplicate. So I signed, because I was getting tired being in that place, and I figured now at last they want my check, and I began writing it again, but the lady said: 'Just a moment, please. Come this way.'

"I followed her to another place where they are allowed to take checks. A person was behind the counter and she took my check and bolted, through a fast-swinging door. I waited, thinking she was in there calling the bank. But she didn't come back.

"The first lady was still near, so I asked her if I was free to go, and she said yes. She was nice, and I liked her all right. I asked her where my lamp was. She said, 'Oh, just take this yellow copy to customer pickup.'

"Up front they told me to get to customer pickup, drive down that street and turn left and watch for the sign. I found the place and a sign said do not park inside the yellow line until my name was called. I parked outside the yellow line. I took my yellow copy inside, and there was a button to push for service. A person came and looked at my yellow copy and told me to have a seat and wait.

"After a while my name was called. I went back and got my car and backed up to the loading ramp, and pretty soon here came a guy driving a forklift and there was a cardboard box on it about a foot and a half tall. My lamp was in there.

"I told the fellow just hand it out to me, and he said, 'Oh, no, I'll load it for you,' and he did. A young fellow weighing maybe two hundred pounds. I could have carried that box out of the store under my left arm, the one where I have arthritis so bad. Now, I wonder if you will agree this is all very strange."

I agreed it was pretty strange.

A Lifetime of Hope

She was a saver, but I don't mean money. During her life there was never any money left to save at the end of a month.

She collected and saved mostly small things that could be packed in cardboard boxes and piled into an old trailer behind an older car. Because they were forever moving. Looking for something better. Or more often, something cheaper.

The things she saved reflected what directed her life—hope, and the certainty that things would surely get better, that her hope was justified.

Her life demonstrated that hope is essential, that living without it is no life at all. A great many mothers of her time lived that way, and probably some still do.

But long after she died I learned something more from her—that hope, even unfulfilled, can amount to a contribution, a gift to others.

After her funeral we stored what she had saved, stacked the boxes in a narrow garage behind the last house they rented, and when we had time we met there, and went through her things.

All her hope was represented (buried, as I thought then) in that dim, dusty place, and going through her savings was a wrenching sadness. Part of the sadness was that she didn't hope for much. A home of her own, that was the main thing. Not a fancy one, either. Just a modest house, with a little yard where she could have a garden and flowers and her grandchildren could come there and play and later they would remember it.

All the saved things we went through in that little garage were for the home she hoped for. Some must have traveled thousands of miles in their boxes, and never got unpacked.

Most of the things were familiar to my sisters but unknown to me. I knew about the shells, though, because I watched her acquire them.

When my son was born she came down from West Texas to see him and I took her to Galveston, to Stewart Beach. That was the first time she had ever been on a salt-water shore.

She was a child, on that beach. She plodded barefoot for a mile in the wet sand and laughed when the surf splashed on her skirt. She gathered shells and we brought them back in a grocery sack.

A few years later I heard her mention those shells. She was lying in the hospital where she died and she said the shells would be nice in the fish bowl.

Coming across what was left of those shells in a sack, in that dreary garage, was a tough moment.

But wounds to the spirit like this, they do heal.

Just lately I've had to move my place of living and that woman spoke to me, again. I was about to walk out of the old apartment where I've lived for twelve years. I turned and looked back and I could see she wouldn't have liked it.

Long ago when we moved out of a place—there were dozens of them—she would repeat the rule: "We're going to leave it cleaner than we found it."

So what I remember about moving is a chore she called scrubbing the woodwork. That meant you got a pan of soapy water and a rag and you washed door frames, window sills and floors, and anything else that might show we had been there and could be washed away by soap and water and elbow grease.

If you asked her why go to all that trouble to clean a place we were leaving, she would say that when we owned our own house, and if we had to leave and rent to somebody else, we would want them to keep it nice.

She never got her own house but she did clean many that belonged to others and left them better than she found them. Not just scrubbed but painted, and patched up, with grass planted, and flower beds fixed, and sometimes trees.

I remember times when we'd go back to places we'd lived so she could see things she had done, years before. "Look at my elm that I planted, how it's grown, and see how nice they've kept the house."

So now I think not that her life was such a sadness but that she spent it spreading cleanliness, and order, and natural beauty to lots of places that were ugly when she came to them. Because of the devout hope that was in her that she would one day have her own home.

I think of her life now as meaning almost the same thing as hope. ○ᴠ

A Little Help

*M*aybe you've witnessed similar scenes. I have, many times, and I'm forever amazed by them.

There's this party, let's say, and everybody is talking and joking and one of the women says to her husband, "Honey, tell 'em about going to the store with Larry."

Her husband says, "Naw, I don't want to tell that."

But the wife is insistent. "Come on, honey. It was so funny."

"You tell it," says the husband. "You were there."

"But I can't tell it the way you do. Come on."

"Oh, all right, I'll tell it. Well, Larry was in town, you know, and he had this camera he'd bought and he needed to . . ."

Wife interrupts. "Larry's a friend of ours, and he travels. He went to school with Joe and when he comes to town he stays with us, and he bought this little camera. Excuse me, honey, go ahead."

"Do you want to tell it?"

"No, I was just explaining Larry, that's all. Go ahead. He bought this camera."

"He bought this camera and it had something the matter with it, so we stopped at the store and . . ."

"It was the little do-jigger that you push," says the wife.

"What?"

"The little thing-uh-mah-jig, to make it snap a picture. It

was jammed or something. I mean that's what the matter was. With the camera."

"Oh. Okay. Anyhow, all three of us went in together and stood around there waiting and waiting and no clerk showed up and finally Larry . . . "

Enter the wife again. "Actually, I wanted to get some film."

Husband stares at her. "What's that got to do with anything?"

"Nothing. I was just explaining why I went in the store. And listen, honey, you didn't say that Larry had bought the camera at that particular store, the last time he was in town."

"Well, of *course* he bought it at that store," says the husband. "He wouldn't be taking it back to a store where he didn't buy it, would he?"

"I guess not. Well, go on."

"Okay. Where was I?"

"We were standing in the store, and nobody came to wait on us and then all of a sudden Larry yelled, and said what he said. Tell 'em what he said, honey."

"*You* tell 'em," growls the husband "You're the one who remembers everything."

"No, I won't do it right. You tell 'em. Go ahead."

"Well, he stood in the middle of the store and put his hands up to his mouth, like this, and yelled, 'DOES ANYBODY WORK HERE?' "

The wife, laughing. "Actually, he said hello first. You know, like you're in a big empty place and you wonder if anybody else is in there and you shout 'hello, hello?' Then he yelled did anybody work there. It was the funniest thing. Go ahead, honey—you know, about the dog."

Husband says, "Okay, so we're all standing there laughing our heads off at Larry, and all of a sudden this little old short-legged mutt comes trotting down the aisle and stops, and stands there wagging his tail, and . . ."

The wife again. "I'm telling you, I thought I'd die laughing. It was the funniest *thing*. I guess what made it so funny, the dog just came right up to us, and looked at Larry, and it was like he was about to ask may I help you or something. I mean like he was a clerk, you know? Honey, tell 'em what Larry did then. You won't believe this."

"You tell it."

"No, I can't tell it right. Go ahead."

"Well, Larry sits down on the floor, see, just sits right down, in front of this little dog . . .."

"It was brown," the wife says. "With white spots."

"What's that got to do with anything?" asks the husband.

"It was just the color of the dog."

"The color of the dog hasn't got anything to do with the story."

"Well, all right, go ahead. But it was a brown and white dog, just the same."

Husband snarls. "So it was brown and white. And had four legs. And a tail, Okay?"

"There's no need to be ugly. Go ahead."

"Well, so finally here comes the storekeeper, and here's Larry sitting on the floor showing this camera to the dog and asking for a refund or something and the storekeeper asks what's happening and . . . "

"No, wait, honey," says the wife. "Actually the store man asked if there was a problem and Larry said no, he'd just returned the bad camera to the only clerk he could find in the place and all he needed now was a $72.68 refund. I thought I'd die laughing. You know?"   ∾

Deep Tractor Thoughts

*L*ast Sunday afternoon I spent three hours on a riding lawn mower. I got quite a lot done, and the grass got mowed in the bargain.

You see a guy chugging along on a riding mower you may guess that he's about to have his brains bored out, but maybe not. He might be working out some kind of troublesome problem that's been keeping him awake.

My theory is that the drone of the engine provides a good background for thinking. It pretty well shuts out distractions, and its constant pitch tends to keep thought on course. As opposed, say, to music. I see people on tractors or mowers listening to these battery-driven tape players. If I listened to music while mowing I wouldn't get much thinking done. All I'd do is sit there creating images of the musicians playing, and the singers singing. Might as well be watching them on television. I don't believe I ever had a creative thought while watching TV.

Back in the spring of '42, I got a job riding a tractor up in the Panhandle, in that wheat and cow country south of Amarillo. All I did for two months, from sunup until sundown, was ride a tractor and pull a disc plow, breaking land to plant feed.

The first three weeks I was sick with boredom. Once you got the discs set right, pulling that plow didn't require a lot of skill. Sometimes you'd be in a field so big you'd need almost half an hour to plow a swath from one end to the other. You watched constantly for diversions. A good one would be a displaced woodpecker flying across your path, hoping he'd find a rotten fence post in the next county.

I tried some displacement of my own, to keep from going nuts. I'd rise off that tractor seat in my imagination and fly with the buzzards. I'd knock home runs in Yankee Stadium. Get shipwrecked on Pacific islands with twenty beautiful girls. I'd compose bad songs, taking the pitch from the tractor engine's tone. I'd sing, sometimes loud as I could manage, confident nobody in that empty land could hear me, and I pray now that nobody did.

When I finally got tired of that stuff, it occurred to me I might do a little planning. I began by planning how I would spend the money I'd get for plowing. I made a list of what I wanted, and went through and marked off what I wouldn't be able to afford. And in that way I had at least the beginning of a system of values.

Then I began thinking about the next few years of my life, and what I intended to do with them, and I was surprised that when I sat there on that tractor seat and thought, calmly, I came up with some really valuable notions.

But it didn't hit me then that for the first time in my life, I was thinking in a straight line about things I needed to think about. Nobody had ever even suggested to me that I needed to learn how to think.

The pity of all this was, as quick as I got away from that tractor and back among people, I stopped having those thought sessions with myself, and I believe it must have been ten years at least before I ever got back to them. And when I started it again, look where I was—driving down the road in a Ford car, on lonesome Texas highways that are a lot like those long straight furrows up there in the Panhandle.

Just every now and then I can get that kind of process going again, and to me it's of considerable value. Sunday afternoon in three hours on that mower I roughed in a chapter of a novel I'm working on. And I wrote a good deal of this piece for today's paper. The yard looks a lot better, too.   ∾

The Iceberg

*Y*ou are talking to an amateur photographer who has been burning film for fifty years to get only a few special shots worth saving. One is the picture of the iceberg which stays tacked to the wall above my desk.

I count this the best photo of an inanimate object I ever got, despite that it's a tiny bit out of focus and the light was coming in at the wrong angle. Professional photographer friends tell me it's not much of a shot, but their standards are different from mine. The main thing I ask for a picture is that it take me back, so I can feel what I was feeling when I punched the shutter button.

When I took the iceberg's picture I was on a boat, and I was cold. I can look at it now, with the temperature on the front porch at ninety-eight, and feel cold again.

That iceberg melted, long ago. It was melting when I took its picture. The melt blended with the salt water of the North Atlantic and no telling where it is now. Some of it may have been in the warm wave that washed over your bare feet last week on a Galveston Island beach.

That was the only iceberg I ever met and I thought it was beautiful. I was on this boat with a bunch of other outlanders and we were chugging around in Trinity Bay, off the coast of Newfoundland.

This was when dog days were going on here at home, so even the waters of Newfoundland's east coast were not being kind to icebergs. This one had drifted down probably out of Baffin Bay, and it had gone aground. It was the size of a ten-story building, and one of the most beautiful and mysterious creatures I ever got near.

I felt it was a living thing, standing there dying, and looking so elegant, so white and splendid.

The young skipper of that boat launched a rubber raft with a ten-horse outboard and put a couple of us in it, and we motored out there and got close to the iceberg. Close enough to reach out and touch.

And look inside it. When the waves came and sucked water away from the base we could look in there and see the rooms with rainbow walls that the warm water had sculptured in the ice.

Then when the water gushed back into the rooms it pushed out frigid air.

Pieces of the iceberg would fall off, and on the way back to the big boat we fished out a chunk of it, about nine pounds, and took it back to the hotel and the cook used it that night to fix our drinks. No, it wasn't salty. It was fresh-water ice, and air was trapped in it, and in your glass it would fizz like soda.

I never have told this before because it seems foolish, but I decided to bring a piece of that iceberg back to Houston. I had a little styro chest, hold maybe a six-pack if you didn't put in much ice. I got about a two-pound chunk off that iceberg piece and wrapped it in newspaper and packed ice around it in the chest. I put it beside me on the seat of the rental car and drove five hours from way up on Trinity Bay to the airport at St. Johns.

I enjoyed thinking about getting home with a piece of

Canadian iceberg in my freezer, so I could show it and say to visitors, "Guess where this ice came from."

Maybe I would have made it all the way, except at St. Johns I had to prove nothing but a piece of iceberg was in my carry-on chest, and unwrapping it didn't help its condition. Time we landed at Boston I had less than a pound of it left.

Then I missed the flight to Houston and had to spend the night in Boston and that's where my iceberg died. I poured out its remains in the airport restroom.

But it still lives, in the picture I took. On these dog days I look up at that photo, tacked to the bulletin board here above my desk, and it helps me stay cool.   ❦

A Deadline, Please

*A*long with one of my *Chronicle* co-workers, I have been involved several weeks in a book project.

We are each assigned to produce, for a book soon to be published, a contribution of about 1,500 words. This has caused both of us a considerable lot of anxiety, and I would now like to tell you why. It might help me to tell it.

I am not going to name my colleague here, because I don't want to embarrass him. To me it doesn't matter. I have been embarrassed so many times over the past forty years it causes no pain any more—or at least not much.

Now then. An assignment to produce 1,500 words is not normally a huge proposition for a journalist. This column you're reading will run probably eight hundred words, maybe eight hundred and fifty. I haven't counted words in a long time. The computer knows when I've used up my space and tells me to stop.

So why has this 1,500-word assignment in connection with a book caused my colleague and me so much misery?

Because they didn't give us a deadline.

As far as I know, there is no record in journalistic history of a newspaperman completing an assignment without a deadline.

The book publisher told us to set our own deadline, and we

did. I have forgotten what the first one we set was. I believe it was last November first. So it must have been about November third that my colleague called and asked if I had written my piece.

I told him I had started but I hadn't finished. I asked if he had written his. Same thing, he said. Started but hadn't finished. What that exchange meant was that neither of us had started at all.

We set a new deadline. November fifteenth.

On November seventeenth I called him to see how he was coming along. He said he had an outline done, and a rough draft. I told him I had done my outline long ago. Actually I had done no outline, and haven't yet, but I didn't want him to think he was ahead of me.

We set another deadline. After Thanksgiving.

Don't you love that for a deadline? After Thanksgiving. That could mean next Fourth of July.

Understand we are talking about a couple of dudes whose very lives are controlled by deadlines. We make deadlines all the time. We have to, in order to get our work done and collect our pay.

But those are deadlines set by somebody else, and that's different.

After Thanksgiving we talked again. I told him I was just about through. He said he was, too. He asked if I wanted to hear some of what he had written. I said go ahead, because we need to be sure we don't both write the same stuff.

He read what sounded like two paragraphs, and stopped. I told him that sounded fine, but I said to myself I bet you a river bottom farm those two grafs are all he's written. Which, if so, was two grafs more than I'd done.

I then told him a story. I am older, and so he listened, or

seemed to. I explained to him the vast difference between newspaper deadlines and book deadlines.

Back in 1964 I signed a contract with a New York publisher to do a book and they gave me a year to write it. I had already been living with daily newspaper deadlines for fifteen years, so I laughed about a deadline twelve months in the future.

One day I looked at the calendar and saw I had three months left to do an entire book of 100,000 words. I went to work on it. I worked nights. Weekends. Holidays. I was supposed to send the manuscript to New York by January first. I didn't even go to a New Year's Eve party. Instead I worked on that book.

But I didn't make the deadline. I didn't finish until the first of February.

In the newspaper business, a deadline means what it says. If you miss a newspaper deadline by a month, they will figure you have died and take you off the payroll.

I supposed that book was a dead pigeon but I sent the manuscript up there anyhow, to see what would happen. In return I got a telegram congratulating me for "making the deadline." They said some writers are years late with book manuscripts.

All this I told to my confederate at the *Chronicle* and he seemed encouraged.

We set a new deadline—December first.

When I saw neither of us would make that one, I called the person in charge of the book project and told him to give us a deadline because otherwise we'd never get the stuff written. He said December eighteenth, and not a day later.

All right, we'll make that and no sweat. They ought to have told us December eighteenth to begin with.　　　　ｏｗ

Digging for Loot

$\mathcal{T}$he last time I was back in the old hometown for a visit I drove a couple of miles out south of the city limits to see if I could find the house where the train robbers buried the money.

Pulled off the blacktop and got through the barbed wire fence and walked the half mile through the prickly pear and mesquite, watching my step on account of rattlesnakes. We used to kill a lot of rattlers right around there.

At first I couldn't figure why the mesquites hadn't done much growing in all those years, but then I saw they weren't the same trees. The land had been cleared at one time, the mesquites chained down, or bulldozed off. Found some black places where the brush had been pushed up in windrows and burned, years ago.

But the mesquite has come back, thick as ever. Maybe thicker. It's had plenty of time. I last walked across that thicket in August of 1937. Fifty-five years ago this month.

I needed half an hour and a good deal of zigging and zagging to figure out that the house is no longer there. Finally I found a scattering of the flat rocks that made up the low foundation piers. Scrub oaks with trunks three inches in diameter have grown up in dirt that was once under the house, so the old place has been gone a good while.

Burned, probably, when they burned the piles of brush. Not much of the lumber would have been worth saving.

We got the story from the tobacco-chewing domino players on the courthouse square. Here's how it sounded:

"In nineteen and seventeen a couple of old boys stood up the T&P passenger train at a water tank outside of Weatherford and taken $20,000 off it and come a' runnin' west. They holed up that night in an old house out south of town here, and the next day the sheriff in Shackelford County caught 'em goin' through Albany. But they didn't have no money on 'em, and it wasn't ever found. Some say that $20,000 is apt to be still buried out yonder around that old house somewheres."

We knew the house, and we didn't have a project going, so we went home and appropriated picks and shovels and pinch bars and post hole diggers and went out there to find the money. Walked, you understand, lugging all those tools.

It wasn't a very strong story, true, but in those times we didn't require much hard evidence in matters of this kind. All we needed was a couple of hints and we'd go storming off in a cloud of enthusiasm.

I suppose it occurred to us that we might go to the newspaper office and find out whether any such train robbery really happened. What would $20,000 in cash be doing riding a passenger train across West Texas? If the robbers brought the money to the house, why would they leave it there and run on west?

It took me years to understand why we didn't ask such questions. It was because we wanted the story to be true, and if we went around asking questions we might find out it wasn't.

The house was a small four-room structure, frame, unpainted, and long deserted. Our country had lots of rural houses like that, and few of their owners seemed to care what happened to them. We used to roam all summer over that dry brushy land and go in and out of deserted houses, exploring, just messing around, and nobody ever paid any attention to us.

That money-hunting adventure lasted most of an arid August. Hot work. Ripping up rotten flooring. Digging. Searching. We looked for metal containers. For some reason we decided the robbers would stick the money in syrup buckets. So our hearts would leap when a pick or a shovel struck anything that sounded metallic. Like a rusty nail, or a lid off a lard can.

It wasn't all work. There were diversions. There were wasps and yellowjackets to fight. Snakes and lizards to kill. Nearby stock tanks that needed swimming in. Rock-chunking contests. And long rest breaks in the middle of the afternoon when we'd lay in the shade and decide how we'd spend the money.

I think that odyssey began coming to a close when somebody's father wondered where his post hole diggers went. And then September came, and school started.

When I revisited the spot not long ago, I treated myself to the thought that maybe the money is really there. If so, I suppose by now even the syrup buckets are rusted to pieces, and the bills turned to dust. ❧

Requiem

Now and then a few of the customers fuss at me because I don't do my work the way I once did. They want me to go back to traveling all the time, keeping to the back roads, talking to bums under bridges and horseshoe pitchers in country towns and nice old ladies who make quilts.

The truth is I simply burned out on all that travel. It stopped being fun.

Something else that tends to keep me off the road is a sadness I feel when I return to all the little towns where I used to work. Going back tends to make me melancholy, since so many of the people I knew in those places are gone. Or else they're old and sick, which is worse.

What kept me happy in that sort of work for so long was a set of contacts who became the finest friends. Seeing them every few weeks was like going home, where I knew somebody would be glad I came back.

When I'm on the highway, sometimes their names sound off in my head, a sonorous roll call:

Dewey Rickbrode, Surfside; Arch Fullinjim, Kountze; Blackie Clark, Richmond; Pud Joines, Glen Flora; Cayce Moore, Hearne; Franz Zeiske, Bellville; Rex Fuller, Brenham; Frank Wardlaw, College Station; Buck Schiwetz, Cuero; Paul Durham, Diboll; Merc Smith, Olivia; Basil Barbee, Nacogdoches.

And then on days when the white perch might be biting on those East Texas lakes, I hear the names of my old fishing buddies at Huntsville:

Freddie Smith, Tex Hardy, John Brannen.

Back in the sixties, Tex and John and Freddie would wait for me to meet my one o'clock class at Sam Houston State, where I was making a little extra money by posing as a journalism instructor.

We'd go up to Sam Rayburn and have these contests on who could catch the biggest crappie, and we'd come home with an ice chest full of fish and give them away. That was the best part—giving away fish to people who were hungry.

There were many others, but I called those names on the roll above because they are gone. All dead.

A couple of them departed just recently—Pud Joines and Blackie Clark.

Frances "Pud" Joines, eighty-four, of Glen Flora, Texas. I wouldn't hope to have a better friend.

When I met her in the early fifties she was third in command of what was called Scheller's Place, in the little Wharton County town of Glen Flora there on the Colorado River. Ed Scheller and his wife, Florence—we called her Mama Dick for a reason I forget—owned Scheller's then, and I worked out of there many days. It was a sort of cafe, but mostly it was a beer joint. No shootings, though. No ugly talk. No nasty behavior. A sedate beer joint.

When Mama Dick and Ed died, Pud took over the place and made it even better, by just being herself. Feeding hungry folks who walked up. Telling stories. Keeping a fine journal on the events that mattered to her.

The journal covered what she cooked for dinner. Who came in and what they said. Who got married. Who had babies. Who had the biggest corn crop there in the Colorado bottom. It was wonderful folk history, recorded in a unique style, and I hope somebody among the relatives has that journal and keeps it safe.

Then Blackie Clark, who died a few days ahead of Pud.

Blackie lived in a trailer house underneath a grove of pecan trees, on the bank of the Brazos at Richmond. He lived to be pretty close to ninety. He was the best storyteller I've ever known, and I don't mind saying I've sat and listened to a mighty lot of them.

Some people outlive their time, so that nobody still alive quite understands that they were extraordinary, that they did things that nobody can ever do again because the things aren't done any longer.

I could write this entire page ten times over about the life of Blackie Clark, or Pud Joines, or Cayce Moore, or Frank Wardlaw or any of those people on the roll call up there. But I'm not sure how many of the current customers would care to hear about it.

People like that may be out there now, but somebody else will have to find them.   ᧁ

Let Sleeping
Panthers Lie

My friend B.J. from up in Cherokee County was back in town early this week to get his annual medical checkup. I talked him in to telling me again the story about how he once spent the night with a panther in the Angelina River bottom.

Took me a good long while to get him tuned up. Says he doesn't like to tell the story any longer because nobody believes it. Then he agreed to tell it again if I wouldn't put it in the paper. But a story is no good to me if I can't put it in the paper, so finally I promised not to use his name.

What follows is exactly the way B.J. told the story, the best I could get it recorded. (When I can't resist a comment during the telling, I'll put it in parentheses, like this.)

"Well, we're talkin' about 1922," B.J. said, beginning the story. "I was fifteen then, and we were livin' in Nacogdoches County, close to Etoile. Papa was farmin' a place on the Angelina, or tryin' to. That place is under water now, on the bottom of Rayburn Lake."

(I wish you could see him, eighty-four years old, long-legged and gray and leather-faced, sitting there chewing on his pipe. He hasn't put tobacco in that pipe for ten years but he still needs it in his mouth.)

"Papa sent me one day to some neighbors," B.J. went on, "for salt. We had a little mare I'd ride for things like this but she came up lame and I had to walk. It wasn't much of a walk. Maybe six miles. Twelve miles round trip.

"Papa told me when I left, he said, 'Now you get your pants back here before dark. Don't you stop and mess around.' I was pretty bad then about messin' around, chunkin' snakes, fightin' bumblebees, whatever turned up. On the way back I had ten pounds of salt in a sack, not much of a load, and I was walkin' along through the woods, sort of daydreamin', and I had this notion that somethin' was behind me. You know how you'll do. Like in church, or in the picture show, you think somebody's tryin' to get your attention so you want to turn around, and look.

"Well, I looked, and there was this panther paddin' along behind me. Big old panther. Biggest one I ever saw. I expect it was ten feet, you count the tail.

"First thing I wanted to do was run. But Papa'd always told me, 'You get a panther on your trail, don't run. Just walk along normal. You try to run, that cat'll get you.'

"I reckon I walked for two miles, with that panther followin' behind me. I'd speed up, and it would too. I'd slow down, it slowed down. It wouldn't get closer to me but it wouldn't go away, either."

(I've read and heard a lot of panther stories, from back when those great animals populated this entire state. Panther, puma, mountain lion—all the same animal. Panthers following people through the wilderness is a common thread in tales about these cats.)

"I decided I might ditch that panther," B.J. said. "There was this kind of trail we were walkin' on, and when I got around a curve I ducked off and ran down a little swale and lay behind some brush. I stayed there a long time, and didn't even raise my head. I stayed until pretty nearly sundown.

"Well, when I looked up, there was that panther, sittin' about fifteen feet away, lookin' at me. I had a big pine just behind me but Papa'd always said, 'Ain't no use climbin' no trees to get away from panthers. They climb trees like squirrels do.'

"If I made a little move, panther made a little move. If I shifted to the right, panther shifted to the right. I decided, well, I'm just gonna keep still, because that's what this panther wants me to do, and I did.

"I reckon it must have been two o'clock in the mornin' before I finally just went off to sleep, because I couldn't keep my eyes open, not even with that big cat lyin' over there lookin' at me."

(I've been collecting panther stories for forty years. I've heard of panthers stealing babies and hiding them unharmed in piles of leaves, and curious stuff like that. But I never heard this one before.)

"I woke up just before daylight," B.J. said, "and that cat was lyin' asleep not six feet from my foot. When I moved, it hopped up and went trottin' off in the woods. Only thing I could ever figure, it just wanted to be close to a person, and sleep.

"When I got on home about sunup Papa said to me, 'What kind of nonsense you been up to all night, boy?' I wanted to tell him the truth, but I was afraid to." ❧

A Valuable Job

$\mathcal{T}$he job I have now, if you want to talk about jobs, is the best I ever had, but I had one in 1937 that I liked almost as much. That was the year I rode a bicycle around the streets of my old hometown and delivered telegrams for Western Union.

The pay wasn't much, but I loved the work. They gave me the sign to put on my bike, that neat Western Union sign with white letters on the blue background, and I wore a Western Union cap.

I went into places few other guys of my bunch were privileged to go. Into the living rooms of the richest people in an important city of 3,000 citizens. Into offices of judges, lawyers, bankers. I could walk right up to the desks of the most successful merchants. I could go in the office of the football coach who was the most important person in our town.

The most feared person in my universe then was the principal of the high school, and if I got summoned to appear before him when school was in session I would shuffle into his office with trembly knees and thumping heart.

But not when I was on the job, wearing my Western Union cap. I could have swaggered in. I never did, but I thought about it.

Our office was half a block off the courthouse square and

next door to the hotel, near the center of our town's doings. I liked being there, listening, keeping my mouth shut, finding things out.

Sometimes I stood behind the operator and watched the words come off the wire, and watched him cut the tape and glue it on the message paper and put it in the envelope that I carried in my shirt pocket when I made deliveries on my bicycle.

Most of the time I knew what the message was. I knew whose grandmother had died, and who'd had a baby in a distant town, and who was out of luck somewhere and was wiring home for money. If the preacher's son wired that he'd been in a wreck, I knew it before the preacher did.

In addition to delivering wires I swept the office and carried out the trash, and sometimes when the operator was busy I answered the phone and told the world what time of day it was. People often called Western Union to get the correct time because it had the great clock on the back wall and it was thought to be the only clock in town that couldn't be wrong.

Citizens who could look out their window and see the courthouse clock counted that time to be the official time, but what they didn't know is that the keeper of the courthouse clock often called Western Union for the exact minute and second. So did the tailor shop, which had a steam whistle it blew at noon and at five o'clock. So did the power plant, which had a great whistle. So did the city hall where the fire whistle was.

After I had given out Western Union time on the telephone for a while, it struck me that I was in a position of power. What if I gave out the wrong time? I could change the time people ate their lunch, because many workers in that town went to lunch when the twelve o'clock whistle blew. I could change the life of that town. I could make people go to work later, or earlier, because they would check the courthouse clock and it would be showing not Western Union time, or county time, but my time, the time I wanted to give out on the telephone.

That nutty notion led to the first story I ever wrote, a bad piece of fiction, a short story I intended to sell to the *Saturday Evening Post* for $300 and buy myself a car. It was about a kid who took over a Western Union office and got control of an entire town by changing all its clocks.

I let the story lay around a couple of weeks, long enough for it to cure out and show faults so grave that even I could see them. I pitched it in the trash, where it belonged.

The most valuable thing I learned in that job came from watching the operator help customers compose the messages they wanted to send. Sometimes laborers out of the oil fields or off poor thin-soiled farms would come in, frowning and worried, needing to communicate with families concerning some emergency.

But they wouldn't reach for a pencil and a message pad because they were illiterate, and the operator would talk to them about what they needed to say, and he would compose a cryptic message and try to get it into ten words or less. I remember the pain on the faces of those men who looked at the operator's words. Maybe no other words would ever be as important to them in all their lives, and they didn't know what they meant.

That would have been a valuable job to have, even if I'd worked for no pay. ‿

The First Notes

*Y*ou might be surprised, as I am, by the range of topics discussed by the regular customers at neighborhood icehouses.

Drive by one of those establishments, with its broad open front, and you look in and see the customers sipping cool ones at the tables and you figure they're talking about sports, or hunting, or barbecues, or local gossip.

But that's not always the case. I've heard some pretty sharp political debates in icehouses, and a few speeches worth hearing on morality, about what's right and what's not. The other afternoon at my neighborhood water hole the regulars were talking about who invented music. Something I'd never thought about.

I didn't take part in that powwow because I had to rush on to somewhere I needed to be. But I carried the question with me, and couldn't get rid of it. Music couldn't have been invented like the steam engine. It had to be what—created? Like fire? And then discovered?

When I got home I dug into the encyclopedia, which is a recent edition, to see what educated people have to say about music's beginning. I was disappointed. Here's *Britannica* quoting Aristotle, "It is not easy to determine the nature of music or why anyone should have a knowledge of it." Way to go, Aristotle.

I looked other places and nobody I've read wants to talk about what I want to know on this matter. They write about music in Asia, in China, and ancient Greece. But how did it originate? Who heard music first? What or who made it happen, this art which has the power to move the human spirit?

OK, I'm on deadline here and can't find anybody to answer my questions so I'll answer them myself. Stand back.

Music began in nature, I'm pretty sure of that. The wind, probably, blowing through branches and grass. And the first song was surely sung by some prehistoric bird.

But I'm interested in human music, and I have sat right here in Houston, Texas and I've seen in a minute how it came to pass.

This person, this ancient creature, sits by the side of a lake somewhere over in the Middle East, or maybe in Africa. I see that it's a male, though a mighty early model of humanity. Truth is it looks more like an ape than anything else but never mind, let's don't get into that.

This dude is feeding on a kind of cane common in that region. The pulp inside the stem is sweet, something like modern sugar cane. He sucks the pulp from a joint of the cane. It happens that a borer, the larval stage of a prehistoric moth, has gnawed two small holes in the wall of this particular cane joint.

All right, now: Probably on impulse, though there is no telling exactly why, when all the pulp is sucked out, this guy blows into the empty cane joint, and produces a whistle. He is pleased by this sound, and gets up and goes clodding around the lake shore, blowing his whistle, making that one note. Everybody thinks he is pretty smart.

Then one day, by accident, while blowing the whistle he puts a finger on one of the holes in the joint and this changes the tone. Say it falls from middle C, as on a piano, down to A.

Every creature in the tribe hears this and is thrilled by the sound, as they should be, since they have heard the first two musical notes ever produced on an instrument by a human.

Those two notes became a song for the colony. Every citizen went around singing them. C to A. C to A. They knew no other notes. (Parents today use these same two notes in calling their children.)

Then two prehistoric mothers in that tribe discovered something even more wonderful. One day, while singing the two-note song, one woman sung an A while another nearby was singing C, and those two notes sung together produced a sound ten times more pleasing than either of the notes made when sung singly.

The entire tribe paused to listen in wonder at the beauty of this sound—the first human musical harmony.

So that's how it all began, and I doubt you will find this history anywhere other than right here in your daily paper.   ∾

A Fire Ant Tutorial

*Y*our attention, please. Will the class kindly come to order, here on the front porch of the old country house in Washington County.

The lesson for today begins on page 122 of our text, "Adventures With Fire Ants." This is Chapter VI, which is titled "Clothing Invaded." I suggest you take notes because much of this material is certain to appear on the next test.

To bring our lesson into focus, let's make an imaginary foray into a patch of native woods. The person taking this stroll is you, and we are assuming you have never met a fire ant.

Say you walk into a stand of oak and cedar, a combination common here in Washington County. You are in search of native flora you want to dig up, take home, and plant in your yard.

Suppose you're interested in live oak saplings. So you find a likely specimen, and you start digging, and it's no cinch to dig up. Takes you three times longer than you thought.

Therefore, while you're digging, you feel a peculiar pin-prick of pain on the calf of your right leg. You have received your first fire ant sting. And it doesn't much impress you. You have endured far greater discomfort, so you ignore the sting and keep digging.

Presently you notice a second pin-prick, not far from where

you felt the first. And not half a minute later you get a third, and this one is over here on your left leg, and higher than the first.

You pause to reflect, and during your reflection two more stings announce themselves, and one is a short distance above your left knee. You may wonder what is going on here. While you wonder, three more stings are delivered and all three are above the knee. They are moving up, and this is important.

At last you'll understand that you have been invaded, and you need to take what we call remedial steps. The first step is to get away from wherever you have been, because you've been on a fire ant bed, or near one, and those vicious little suckers have crawled up your legs.

Now, the best way to kill a fire ant, despite the recommendations you have heard from our state's foremost entomologists, is to squash the miserable thing between your thumb and forefinger. This course is effective if you have no more than six ants in your clothing.

What you do, you stand quietly and wait for the stings to begin again. A fire ant is not like certain other small stinging creatures that gasp and die after they discharge fire, their only ammunition. A fire ant will wander around in your pants half the day and pop you every time it finds a likely spot.

Say you've got on jeans, the common wear for walking in woods. So you stand waiting, and when the next sting occurs you grab at where it hurts and pinch the location with the forefinger and thumb and hope you smash the ant through the material.

If it doesn't sting you again, assume you did smash it. If it does sting you again, give it another pinch. You may need three pinches.

If you still miss, spread your hand and rub the area violently.

Heat generated by the friction sometimes gets the ant when a pinch misses it.

Understand that while you are pinching or rubbing to death one fire ant on the side of your left thigh, two others may be asking for a pinch on the back of your right knee, a location known to fire ants as an especially fruitful target.

Remember this: A fire ant loves to die. Dying is its purpose for being. Because as quick as you smash it, it is reincarnated as two fire ants instead of one. This is what I think. My belief has not yet been supported by all the fire ant research going on at public expense. But I bet it will be, in the end.

If you are standing out there in the woods, and feeling more than six stings at once, your next step is to take your pants off and do an inventory. This means turning your jeans inside out and getting those little felons out of there. Because if half a dozen of them are already stinging your legs, at least four more are probably coming up below them. Or worse, above them.

If you realize, in fact, that as many as a dozen fire ants are in your pants, get pantless quick, no matter who is watching.

Because trust me when I say, you don't want to fool around and let twelve fire ants crawl up your legs much higher than mid-thigh. Class dismissed.   ॐ

But She Was a Girl

One of the customers called early Wednesday morning and here's what he said:

"I guess you saw the story in the paper, in the sports section, about that girl out in Los Angeles who pitched the ball game. She was the starter, and lasted nine innings. Pitched for a school out there, Southern California College, and her team won, too.

"Her name is Ila Borders, according to the paper, and she's just eighteen. Good for her, is what I say. But I tell you what, there've been dozens of girls who were good athletes and they could have pitched in college just the same way, but the trouble is they never did get the chance, because they're girls.

"Reason I called, I thought about a girl I grew up with. Her name was Mary Eloise Culpepper, and she was the best athlete I ever knew. I'm not saying she was the best there ever was, but she was the best I ever knew, like I say. I went through school with her.

"Mary Eloise moved into our neighborhood when she was about twelve, and she was already something by then. First time I ever saw her, she was out in the front yard playing catch with her little brother, who was like four years old. By playing catch I mean she was pitching him up in the air and catching him before he hit the ground. He was a tough, chunky little kid and loved rough treatment that way.

"Mary Eloise wasn't especially big but what there was of her, man, it was sure put together. She had long legs and arms and short yellow hair, and she had a pretty face, too, not beautiful but sweet, and this special kind of smile, and the nicest teeth. I remember her teeth.

"Not too long after her family moved into our neighborhood the school had what they called a sports day. On sports day they dismissed all the classes and everybody went out on the football field and ran races. Girls ran against girls and boys ran against boys.

"Well, Mary Eloise won all the girls' races and she won so easy, the track coach called her over and got her to run against his sprinters. I mean the boys, sure. She beat 'em all in the hundred. Coach tried her in the two-twenty and she beat 'em in that, too. I'm talking about a girl twelve or thirteen years old and she's outrunning boys seventeen and eighteen years old.

"When she got up in high school, we had a girls' softball team. My sister played on it. Second base. She said after they'd played three or four games their coach went to the principal and said it wasn't fair for Mary Eloise to be on the team. Principal asked how come, and the coach said when she pitched she fanned all the batters.

"Principal says, 'You mean all the batters? Every one?' Coach says, 'Every one.' Principal says, 'How about when she bats? Can she hit?' Coach says, 'Hits a home run every time she comes up.' You know what they did? Took her off the team. Wouldn't let her play because she was too good for the other girls.

"I was on the baseball team then. Never did start, but sometimes I could come up late and scratch out a base hit and bring in a run so they kept me on the bench, to pinch hit. That's how I got acquainted with Mary Eloise. She started coming around and working out with the team, and she wasn't anything but a sensation.

"She could hit, run bases, scoop up grounders, stab line drives. Had a better arm than our center fielder. Coach went to the principal and said he could sure use Mary Eloise on the baseball team. Principal says nothing doing because she's a girl and might get hurt.

"Coach says, 'Hurt? Only player on my team that's hurt is my shortstop. He got spiked during practice by a runner sliding into second.' Principal says, 'Who spiked him?'

"Coach goes, 'Mary Eloise.'

"But they wouldn't let her play. She ended up kind of an assistant coach. Used to pitch batting practice so I faced her a few times. We didn't have a pitcher who could throw a curve that would stay inside the park but Mary Eloise could wrap one around your neck.

"And she had just a picture-perfect swing at the plate, too. She'd sit with us on the bench at games and when I'd get called up to pinch hit, like in the last inning and the score tied, she'd slap me on the seat of my pants and say 'Go gittum, Tiger,' But I knew. It ought to have been her going up there, not me.

"In that league, Mary Eloise could have gone to the plate in high heels and a silk dress and hit .500. But she was a girl, and didn't get to play." ∾

Copy Pencils and Paste Pots

A young visitor was in my diggings at home, where I write most of this stuff.

He roamed, trying to keep from making noise because there'd been the promise that when I was through, we'd go down to the *Chronicle* and watch the big presses run. I'd offered a trip to the zoo but he chose the presses.

So I was trying to finish, and he came up behind me and asked, "What's this?"

Told him it's a copy pencil.

"What do you use it for?"

I don't use it any more. When I first started out in the newspaper business we used these soft-lead pencils to edit copy. Like when I misspelled a word I could mark through it with this pencil and write in the correct spelling just above it.

"Why do you keep it if you don't use it?" he asked.

On account of sentiment. Same reason he keeps his old toys that he doesn't play with any longer. Somewhere around here I also keep a paste pot.

"A paste pot?" He thought that was funny.

Yes, every newspaper desk used to have a pot of paste and a brush and we pasted the pages of our stories together, end to end. A big story might make a string of paper six or seven feet long. It was a way to make sure the pages stayed in the right order when they were taken to the back shop to be set in type. Long strings of copy paper. I always thought they were beautiful.

"Copy paper?" he said. "You mean like on a Xerox?"

No. That word, copy, was common around newsrooms. Copy paper was just pages of newsprint that we typed our stories on. Then the story itself became what we called copy. A reporter referred to his story as copy, before it was printed.

"But not now?" he asked.

Well, sometimes. But now everything is done on computers and a story when it's being written is called text, which I hate. Or it's called a document, which is worse. I wasn't trained to write documents.

"What's this?" he asked, holding up a gray object.

It's a line of lead type, which I keep for the same reason I keep the other old stuff. That slug is from what old dudes like me call the hot type days.

Used to be that when we wrote a story, it went to the back shop and a Linotype operator tapped on a keyboard and reproduced the story in metal. I loved that. It was like having your words carved in granite, even though the next morning they would be melted into liquid lead again.

"A line-oh-type? What's that?"

Linotype. It's a machine. When the operator keyed words into it they would appear in hot metal and then the metal hardened and it could be locked on a press and inked and the words reproduced on paper. Even today, among all these technical marvels, the Linotype is an extraordinary machine.

"Do you have one?"

Oh no. They're huge, and I wouldn't know where to keep one. I haven't seen a Linotype in years.

"What's this?" he said, and picked up a pink pen.

That's left over from the scanner days. When we stopped typing stories on ordinary paper, we used what they called scanner paper. This was the beginning of the end of the old way of putting out newspapers. The scanner days were terrible.

"Why?" he asked.

Because for the scanner we had to type our stories inside boxes pre-drawn on the paper. Sentences had to begin in a certain place, and end in a certain place. Paragraphs couldn't be ended or begun where you wanted them to end or begin. In my opinion, this is when newspaper editorial employees stopped being mainly reporters and writers and entered into the slavery of technology. I think it wounded whatever artistry was in us and made us technicians, button punchers.

"But what's this pink pen?" he asked, obviously bored with my outburst.

The scanner which reproduced our sentences couldn't read pink so we could write instructions to the printers on our stories and the scanner wouldn't see them.

"Hey, that's cool," he said.

But I thought it was simply weird, carrying pink pens everywhere.

When I got my stuff done and shut the computer down he asked, "Don't you like working on a computer?"

I didn't want to talk about it, without using words he ought not to hear. Told him to put on his jacket and we'd go downtown and watch the big presses run. ∿

Bread, Butter and Sugar

During the coffee hour at the drugstore one of the gents at the counter was moaning about a diet he's on, and how he's hungry all the time, even when he's just finished eating what the diet will let him have.

"All I ever think about now is food," he said. "I've thought about things to eat that I hadn't thought of in forty years. This morning I thought about eating a big hunk of bread, butter and sugar."

I remember that. Long ago in the boondocks we ate bread, butter and sugar between meals to take away that old empty feeling.

Say a kid came home from school thinking he'd surely starve before supper if he didn't eat something. He'd take a slice of bread and slather it with butter and then spoon sugar over the butter. I can remember boys coming out of the house late in the afternoon to play ball and they'd be eating a slice of bread they'd doctored up that way.

I told the fellow at the counter that bread, butter and sugar sounded pretty awful to me now.

He said, "It doesn't to me. I could eat two, right now, but

then I could eat anything. That stuff was supposed to be a snack. No telling how many hundred calories it had."

He held up a thumb with a forefinger lifted above it about an inch, showing a measurement. "Chunk of that bread might be this thick, because we're talking about before sliced bread came along and we'd cut it off a loaf of homemade. Make it thick as you could handle."

Put on all the butter you wanted, too, right?

"Oh yeah." He laughed about the butter. "We'd put it on, I guess a quarter of an inch thick. Nobody cared how much butter you used, not at our house. Only thing Mama ever fussed at me about was using too much sugar. She'd churn every other day so there was always plenty of butter but sugar cost money and you had to go to town for it."

How many calories could have been in one of those chunks of bread, butter and sugar?

"No telling," he said. "All that butter? I bet five hundred calories, easy, and many a day after school I'd eat two of 'em. Still I grew up skinny as a broomstick. Now look at me. Spare tire around my waist, fit a Mack truck."

He finished his coffee, black, no sugar, and went on out and left me thinking about a snack we used to make that sounds even worse than what he put on that bread. We called it cocoa and sugar.

You took a cup and put in a heaping teaspoon of cocoa and then filled the cup maybe half full of sugar and you mixed the cocoa and sugar together and ate it dry, with a spoon. Almost like eating pure sugar.

Gross, yes. And what made it worse, kids would pour a spoon of that stuff inside their lip and let it dissolve and go around grinning, so you could see the sugary chocolate mess in their mouths and it looked like snuff.

Some of these were children of my own generation, who

didn't even own toothbrushes and never had a dentist look inside their mouths until they were grown. Little wonder so many of them had lost half their teeth by then.

The fellow at the drugstore who talked about bread, butter and sugar said his trouble was high cholesterol, and that's why he's on the diet. Early in his and my generation, we didn't know about cholesterol and we committed dietary trespasses that would cause today's doctors and nutritionists to release primal screams.

Here's one I remember. I can still taste it:

Go in the kitchen in the middle of the afternoon. Find a big glass that would hold a pint at least. Put about an inch of chocolate syrup in the bottom. We'd make the syrup with cocoa and sugar. Then fill the glass with pure cream, stir, stand in the middle of the kitchen floor and drink the whole thing down.

Nauseates me to remember it now but I did that many times. Just pure Jersey cream. When the cows were milked the milk was poured up in crocks and left out so the cream would rise, and then the cream was poured off and refrigerated, and it was always there to tempt anybody who opened the ice box.

Back when we were drinking cream and eating bread, butter and sugar we thought it was all right as long as it didn't make us fat. And at the time, it didn't.

Today I may have gained two pounds just writing about it.   ∾

A Pet Turkey

Once upon a time, long ago, before I left the bosom of my family to go forth and seek my fortune, there lived a turkey by the name of Joshua Deuteronomy. His home was a pen in the back yard of our house.

My father, who in those days was always looking for curious projects, brought this bird in from the country where it was hatched. He built a pen for it and bought corn and maize to feed the turkey and he made a speech.

He said my sister and I were to take care of the turkey and feed it and fatten it and when Thanksgiving came we would have a fine bird for our festive meal and it would not cost anywhere near as much as buying a turkey at the grocery store. He said the assignment would teach us a valuable lesson in how responsible labor, performed at home, could turn a handsome profit.

This was a skinny bird with a pitiful look in its eye and therefore my sister loved it at first sight, as she loved all living things that looked pitiful in any way. She is the one who christened the turkey Joshua Deuteronomy.

The reason for that choice, she had just won a New Testament at the Methodist Church for memorizing the names of all the Books of the Bible, and reciting them without a bobble before an assembly of the Sunday School's Intermediate De-

233

partment. She also received a certificate suitable for framing, though it was never framed.

Another name that was in nomination for the bird was Malachi Lamentations and I liked it better but my sister decided Deuteronomy was the most beautiful of words and a pitiful turkey would find comfort in being called by it. She was two years older (still is, in fact) and always won tie votes on seniority.

Even though I had not yet climbed fool's hill at this time, I knew something my father did not, which was that the Thanksgiving turkey-feeding project would fail. My sister would not allow it to succeed.

I had seen her cause failures before. She once ran the family out of the rabbit business. My father had built hutches in the back yard and they were full of rabbits having babies to beat sixty and prospects for this enterprise were favorable.

Then my sister learned that the idea of this enterprise was that we would raise rabbits and sell them to people who would eat them. The day of the first harvest we saw that nothing of this kind could take place on our premises, not if we wanted peace. We passed out of the rabbit business because none of us could stand hearing my sister wail, in grief about those bunnies she had named and loved.

You can see my father was a slow learner in some areas. Even I was faster, in the very areas where he was weak. I knew from the beginning that my sister would never permit that turkey to be slaughtered, and it was not.

The first hint came the second night of that bird's residence with us. A rain came, and my sister went out and got the turkey and brought it in the house.

But Joshua Deuteronomy did thrive, under my sister's constant care. He grew. He gained weight. His feathering became thick and shiny. His wattles red and healthy. And the pitiful look in his eye changed, and I didn't much like the new one. It had a sort of haughty quality.

And why not? My sister carried that bird around under her arm until it got too heavy to lift. She convinced him that he was the finest of all birds. She taught him to strut and gobble on command, and to speak what she called English.

She would ask him, "Who works behind the counter at the dry goods store? And he would answer, 'Clerk, clerk, clerk.'"

The day before Thanksgiving, when Joshua Deuteronomy was scheduled to be slaughtered, my sister was leading him around the neighborhood with a pink ribbon looped gently around his neck. He gobbled for the entertainment of the public, and clerk-clerked in answer to the dry goods store question.

That was the year we had fried chicken for Thanksgiving dinner. I don't recall that my sister grieved about the chickens. Her grief was reserved mainly for creatures she'd been acquainted with personally, and in all the years since this story began, she has not changed. ❧

Go West for Sunsets

*H*ere's a letter from one of the customers, Dustin Hall of Tomball, who wonders where he can go to see a pretty sunset or sunrise in this part of the world.

I understand his problem. Houston is not famous for pretty skies, mainly because our real estate is so flat. This doesn't mean we don't have nice sunsets, though. The trouble is, few of us ever see them because buildings and trees obscure the horizon.

It helps to get a little elevation. I've seen some spectacular sunsets in Houston but not when I was in the front yard. I once saw a dandy from near the top of Transco Tower.

When I read the first few lines of Hall's note I thought all I needed to do was send him to Galveston. One of my passions is sunrise at Galveston, and I've watched dozens of them.

What you do is go down there and spend the night, or else get up so early you can be on Seawall Boulevard at first light. Then you face east and you wait. And wait. And wait. You'll think sunrise is never going to come. You'll say, Hey, this is scary. It's The Day The Sun Didn't Rise.

But finally when that fireball breaks out of the Gulf it climbs fast, as if it's late and trying to make up for lost time.

The best thing about a Galveston sunrise is that even without clouds to provide color, it'll be a show worth watching.

Down lower in Hall's note he said he'd already watched sunrises at Galveston and wanted a more rural setting. Well, you can catch nice sunrises and sunsets almost anywhere in rural Texas but you can't predict whether they'll be especially spectacular. I've seen wonderful sunrises out on the Katy Prairie where the land is flat as the Gulf of Mexico, but you need some help from broken clouds to provide a variety of color and they aren't always there.

For more dependable sky beauty at dawn and sunset, I'd say head west to mountain country. Go out the other side of the Pecos to Big Bend. Or go to New Mexico, around Santa Fe and Taos.

In Santa Fe you can even buy a sunset, without a guarantee. La Fonda, the hotel on the central plaza, has a little bar it opens late in the afternoon, up on the roof. You go up there and sit in a metal chair and buy a drink and watch the sun go down and sometimes the scenery is worth more than the price of the drink.

My experience on that roof says it's a fair gamble. Once in a while the sky is just splendid. Of course you can drive outside town and stop on the side of a mountain and watch, and nobody will try to sell you anything.

The best sunsets I ever saw in Texas were out in the Big Bend Country, back when I was traveling all the time. Go to Alpine and turn left, which from Houston will take only a couple of days. Run on down about eighty miles to Study Butte or Terlingua, find a place to park at the end of the day, look back east, and be patient.

The soft light of the sinking sun on the rocky west wall of the Chisos Mountains produces some of nature's finest artistry. First time I saw it was in the late fifties. I watched it with a geologist I happened to meet. He was living in a mobile home on Ranch Road 170 near Terlingua. Said he'd watched the sun go down hundreds of days, and the colors on the mountainside were different every time.

That Trans-Pecos country is fine for sunrises, as well.

What seems like a century ago I woke up one morning in a camp in McKittrick Canyon, which is now in Guadalupe Mountains National Park. This was before that rugged region became a park. It was a ranch then.

For Texas this is high country, just south of the New Mexico line and not far from Guadalupe Peak, which tops out at 8,751 feet. You can't get higher than that in this state without flying.

The camp where I slept was in the upper end of McKittrick. From that point the canyon snakes down pretty sharply, with lots of stone-walled bends. I woke up before dawn and the cook gave me a cup of coffee and told me where to sit, "to watch the sun come up the canyon."

What he meant was that you could sit in near darkness and look down the canyon and see the sunlight turning those bends, bouncing off the walls, climbing toward you, and it's like watching a flood of fire, surging uphill.

Which was the best sunrise I ever saw. Except maybe for a couple of extra good ones at Galveston.　　　　　ᘉ

A Feel-Good List

$\mathcal{B}$een feeling punk lately? Does the news get you down? Are you fed up with people robbing and killing one another? Is that what your trouble is?

Then maybe what you need to do is make a feel-good list, of things you still like about living on this particular planet.

I make such a list at least once a year and here's my current one:

Corn on the cob, when it's been boiled at the right stage and tastes, and feels, so wonderful when you take the first bite.

Getting a letter or a phone call from a good friend you haven't heard from in twenty years, and he/she is doing well and has no sad story to tell.

Hoot owls, right here in the city. Sunday night I was out on Memorial near Chimney Rock, just after dark, and heard a great horned owl sounding off. This was almost next door to the office building of our foremost citizen. I wonder if former President George Bush has ever heard owls hoot in his neighborhood. I hope he has.

Fresh vegetables for sale. Some of the prettiest sights in this city are in the produce departments of supermarkets. A few of the displays approach works of art. But I wonder whether that sells more vegetables. I walk up to a three-foot-high arrangement of carrots, I'm hesitant to take any out of the stack because it would seem to destroy the creation of the person who produced that vegetative sculpture.

Fresh-squeezed orange juice splashing across the back of the tongue at six o'clock in the morning.

Speaking of six a.m., how about going out for the paper at that hour, just after the first norther of the fall has come in, and you don't want to go back inside. You want to stand out there and take deep breaths and the joggers and the pedal bikers come by and they speak to you when ordinarily they don't. Strangers, sharing something good. "Hey, how about this weather?"

A bill comes in and says you've got a credit and you don't have to send anything this month. This happens. It's happened to me twice in the last thirty years. It could happen to you at any time, so be prepared.

The phone rings and the tiny voice of a grandchild says, "Papa?"

Hurricanes that turn north and blow themselves dead in the Atlantic.

Onions in a skillet, sliced and sizzling in not-too-much olive oil. Gives off one of the finest of all aromas.

Getting my checkbook balanced, or at least close.

Anesthetics. Recently I had a root canal, which is often mentioned as the worst possible way to spend a day. Maybe root canals are getting bad press. They don't hurt, if the one I had is representative. I've had more discomfort during a routine teeth cleaning than I felt during that root canal. They ain't cheap, though. Hoo boy.

Making a good sandwich, and all the makings fit exactly right between the pieces of bread and the first couple of bites taste and feel the way you thought they would.

Being out on the road, going somewhere you especially want to go, and your vehicle runs nice and smooth and when you stop to fill up, you find out you're getting better gas mileage than you expected.

Planting seeds, and they come up fast and look healthy and promising.

Being on your favorite stream, with a fly rod, and you see a bass stirring in shallow water about fifty feet downstream, up against a brushy bank. You get some line flying, and more line, and a little more, and there's no wind and you don't hang up on willows behind you, and when things feel right you release and the line rolls across the water and the fly plips onto the surface in exactly the spot you hoped for, and the fish hits it. This happens to me maybe once in a hundred casts. It's about the only thing that means much to me any longer, about fishing. I don't care how big the fish is. I don't even care if the fish gets free before I land it. I just need to make that perfect cast, and get the strike.

Brewing a good cup of coffee early in the morning, and going out on the porch and holding a mug of it under the nose, and inhaling the aroma. Before you ever take the first sip. Knowing how good it will taste.

Being halfway through a good book, and having time to hide away and finish it.

Going to the doctor with a worrisome symptom, and finding out it doesn't amount to anything.

Drifting off to sleep to the sound of a gentle rain on a tin roof.

Tax refunds and stock splits.

The way your desk looks just after you get it cleared, and everything around it is in the proper place—before you start messing it up again.

Mozart's "Requiem," Billy Joel's "Just the Way You Are," and Waylon Jennings' "What Am I Gonna Do?"

A great flight of sandhill cranes going over, sending down their throaty calls from high altitude.

Your dog flopping down and putting his muzzle gently on your foot.

A sports team you're interested in is the underdog in a big game, and it pulls out a win.

Singing good old songs around the piano with friends.

Putting on a pair of pants you haven't worn for two years, and they still fit.

The silky way your old car runs after it's had a tuneup, a wash and lube, and a new set of tires.

Going through the pockets of a coat and finding the pair of glasses you lost six months ago.

A long sleepy hug, early in the morning, from your favorite person.

Then, finally, writing a decent piece in this space, one I think the customers might enjoy. That's the best feeling of all. Except maybe for the hug.   ∾

Index

Subject Index

Index